ALSO BY TRAVIS WOO

'MAGIC LIFE: MY STORY OF BECOMING A PRO PLAYER'

I WISH I HAD TOLD ME SOONER

I wish I had told me sooner. I wish someone had told me sooner. I wish I had known earlier so I didn't have to spend so much time wandering lost. I wish I had asked more questions. I wish I had asked for more directions. I wish I had found more mentors and read more books. I wish I hadn't wasted so much time. I wish I would have gotten started sooner. I wish I could go back to a younger me and give me this advice, but I can't. Instead I will give you this advice to try to save you from making the same mistakes I made. You can get there way faster than me.

I wasted a lot of time learning by trial and error. I made a lot of mistakes along the way. Sometimes I learned, sometimes I didn't. It wasn't the best approach. It's much better to learn from other's mistakes so you don't have to make them. You can learn from mine and zoom on ahead. That is my goal for you. To get the success you want way sooner. To avoid much of the pain I had to go through. To get a good life with good days as soon as possible.

I don't claim to have it all figured out, but I know a lot more than I knew 10 years ago. I tried a lot

1

of things. I didn't necessarily have the easiest start. My parents were great but they didn't have it all figured out either. There was alcohol and prescription drugs around. Society didn't love me and I had to face bullies. I was small and scrawny. I was sun deficient and cold in Seattle. I was an anxious and twitchy kid. But I had something in me. I knew I wanted to make a difference. I knew there was a better life out there, I just didn't know how or what.

I worked hard in school. I worked hard in athletics. I worked hard in part time jobs. I worked hard in my hobbies. I played competitive card tournaments. I made music and promoted it. I wrote stories. I YouTubed. I had a social life and girlfriends. I read. I tried starting small businesses. I coached athletes. I built my social media brand. I grinded really, really hard. It wasn't always pleasant, but I knew I had to keep going.

Of all the things that could have taken off, it was the combination of card tournaments, content production, and social media that did it. I was invited to play on the Magic: the Gathering Pro Tour and travel Europe, America, and Japan. I earned a blogging job from a premier website that let me set my own hours from anywhere in the world. I was free to experiment.

I tried being a professional competitor. I tried being a traveling content producer. I tried being a serious basketball player in Spain. I tried being a surf bum in England and Mexico. I tried organic farming in

California. I tried starting my own coaching businesses, because I was forced to.

Along the way, I made mistakes on social media. I threw tantrums at my low points. I lashed out at critics. I made enemies. I made drama and caused controversy. I didn't hold my tongue. It blew up in my face. I lost my blogging job which had become the main source of my income. I blew my money in panic. I called my parents but they wouldn't help me.

I was lucky to be offered a place by one of my first bosses and mentors. It was in their basement on a fold out couch. I moved back to Seattle in the winter but was too poor for good warm clothes. My cash situation was bad and my job prospects were nil. I had to start my own business. I worked 10 hours a day online, making products, coaching, marketing services, creating webpages, livestreaming, and making phone calls. When I got off I talked to my mentor, went for quick workout, and read business books into the night. Fortunately, my business took off and I was free to move again. I had a second chance.

I moved back to California and got more into organic agriculture. Of all the lives I tried, this one was the one I enjoyed most. I loved working outside. I loved digging my feet into the soil. I loved the community. I loved eating the food. I loved seeing the food eaten. It mattered. It just felt right.

I decided to play one more card tournament. Out of 1600 players I finished 2nd. There was a moment along the way where I had to draw a specific card, and I did. Maybe it was luck, maybe God was watching over me. I won an invitation to a tournament in Hawaii. I rocked the tournament in Hawaii. I won an invitation to Ireland. I rocked the tournament in Ireland. From there I went to Sweden, France, Spain, Amsterdam, Mexico, Nashville, Richmond, Baltimore, Las Vegas, California, Japan, and back to Hawaii all within the year. I met epic people along the way and lived countless adventures. It was awesome, but I began to burnout.

I took a break from competition to spend months in Hawaii working on organic farming. I was lucky to find a great place for me, referred to it by a card playing friend. I found it to be a better life for me, but I was conflicted by obligations to continue playing professionally. I reluctantly left the farm for another extended globetrotting trip. Early in the trip. I found out I would be suspended from the tour.

This time I was lucky to not learn my lesson. An unmoderated Facebook group I had made blew up over unsavory memes. Politics entered the primary space in the community. The parent company came in and suspended players for social media transgressions on YouTube, Facebook, twitter, and twitch. I was caught in the crossfire. This eliminated my choice. I would go back to Hawaii to farm. Lucky.

I love my life on the farm. The work is hard and meaningful. I spend most of the day outside. The birds sing, the sun shines, the wind blows, the rain pours, the birds sing, the leaves rustle, the sheep bleat, the clouds burst over the mountains, the sun sets over the water. Our team lives and works together in a village. We have youth, passion, and excitement. We grow our own food and eat it together. We share it with the community. There is friction, but it is the way society has been. It's a fine cost. It's a more simple and normal life.

I wish I had gotten here sooner. I could've gotten started on this life 10 years ago. I could have skipped all the wandering. I could have skipped most of the pain and trauma. If I could advise a younger me, I would have. But I can't. I took the slow route. You don't have to though. You can learn from my story and skip to the life you want. It won't happen for you overnight. It might even take you a few years. But it won't take you nearly as long as me. I wish I had told me sooner, but I can't. So I can tell you instead.

THE SEQUENCE TO SUCCESS

There is a sequence to success. There is a step by step order to the good life. If you do things out of order you will at best get there slowly, at worse never get there at all. It's simple. One thing happens after another. Each ingredient builds on the previous. There is a pyramid. You have to start from the foundation. If you go for the top at the beginning, the whole things will collapse. I wish someone had told me this sooner, because I didn't start off in the right order, and it took me much longer to get here than it could have. But you can get here sooner if you follow these steps.

The base of the pyramid is health. Your body is how you experience the world. Your mind is a part of your body. Your emotions, thoughts, and feelings come from your body. Your ability to work and enjoy the fruits of your labor require a body. Your happiness is highly dependent on your body. A sick body feels bad. A good body feels good. Good loving relationships are better with good health. Poor health makes it hard to care for others. So you must start with your health. Love your body. Take care of your parts. Go out of your way to eat the best you can. Exercise. Study the body. Prioritize it above everything. When you are healthy, you can move on to the next step.

After health comes wealth. Money does matter. You have to be able to afford the necessities of shelter and quality food. To eventually support others you must take care of your wealth. Wealth goes way beyond money though. Wealth includes having good hard fulfilling work that gets you out of the bed in the morning. You should have a labor of love. A passion for what you're doing. Your work should be your vehicle of making an impact on the world. To make a difference for being here. For leaving a legacy. If you don't have this, you will feel an emptiness and a loss. You have to be healthy to fulfill your wealth potential. You can't call in sick to your dreams. Once your health is secured, wealth is next. After wealth comes happiness.

You can try to start with happiness, but it's much easier when you are healthy and have your basic needs met. You should try to be as happy as you can with what you have, but there is a certain reality to things. Poor health and poor wealth create stress and bad emotions. They ruin relationships too. You don't need everything, but decent health, some financial security, and fulfilling work will go a long way to your happiness. If you still aren't happy, it's something you can work on. Better mindsets, more gratitude. Different ways of looking at the world, more thanks. Strategies for improving your life through the days and the moments and the people. Proper strategy creates more happiness. Happiness is an intention and it's something you can have more and more of. Once you are relatively happy, the door opens for love relationships.

It's possible to love with nothing, but it's much easier to pour from a full cup. It's much easier to care for others when you are cared for. It's much easier to help other people be healthy when you are healthy. It's much easier to be generous and supportive when your needs are met. It's much easier to share your passion and excitement for the world when you feel it in your work. It's much easier to share your happiness when you are already happy. If you are lacking, deficient, and miserable, you aren't ready for love relationships. They can become toxic, cancerous, and make your lives worse. You must put your oxygen mask on yourself first, then turn to others. When you are healthy, wealthy, and happy, love relationships will come more easily.

That is the sequence to success. You may debate it, but there is a sound logic and some science to it. They all feed into each other. More wealth makes it easier to be healthy. A good loving relationship will boost happiness. It doesn't have to all happen in exact order. These are all things you continue to work on. But if you work on them in the right order and are willing to delay and sacrifice things until you are ready, it will happen much sooner. You will be healthier sooner, wealthier sooner, happier sooner, and have better relationships sooner. You can get there by wandering lost but do it in the right order and you can have the good life fast. I wish someone had told me sooner, but I can tell you right now. So let's go!

HEALTH

PUT YOUR BODY FIRST

Put your body first. Your health comes before anything else. If you aren't healthy you won't have the energy to do a good job, have good relationships, or be happy. If you are healthy you will have the energy to do a great job, have great relationships, and be very happy. This is the foundation of your life. It is your keystone to all things. You must put it before everything else whenever possible. After you've taken care of your health everything else will fall into place much more easily

Put your mental health first. It's easy to forget that your brain is a physical organ in your body. Your brain is made from and fueled by the foods that you eat. And shaped by the workouts and experiences you have. You can easily make yourself smarter as you make yourself fitter, stronger, and more effective. Make decisions that lead to good food and activity, but also meditate, love yourself, and practice affirmations.

You will have to make sacrifices. You will have to spend more money on food. You will have to have the discipline to come home early, shut off the electronics, and go to sleep at a regular hour. You will have to go out every day and challenge yourself physically even when you aren't feeling up to it. You will have to take out time to study the body to better understand how it functions. You will have to sacrifice a lot of to do this.

Putting your body first is like putting your own oxygen mask on first. Once you've done this you will be able to help yourself in other ways. If you try to put on someone else's mask first you could all die. It's not selfish to put your health first, it's necessary. Once the other areas of your life are taken care of you can go help other people- make an impact, make a difference. Once your needs are met you can think about helping other people meet their needs. It's all built on your body. You must put it first. The rest of this section will help you figure out how to best do that.

LOVE YOUR BODY

You are going to have to love yourself and love your body to do all the things necessary to care for yourself in the best way. It's up to you. It's not up to anyone else. It's not up to your parents anymore- you are your own parent! If you need to treat yourself as your own child to nourish yourself, then do that. You will have to go above and beyond, the extra mile, to sacrifice to provide for yourself. If you do this and have time left over you will be able to care for other people.

Thank your body for making it this far. It may not be perfect, it may struggle, it may have problems, but it has walked the steps to get you to this point in life. Maybe things could be better, but things could be much worse if you had given up back then. But now you're here, in a position to make the most of it, because of your body. Love your body. It does all the hard work for you- all that thinking, breathing, sweating. Everything you have ever done is thanks to your body, so take care of it.

Loving your body should be fun but it's also serious business. The body is all you really have. When it's gone, you lose everything else. It's special to get a body. Most potential people are never born. Billions of sperm never find an egg. It's a miracle that you're here and you ought to make the most of it. It's a special privilege to have a body at all and you should appreciate that. Love yourself, love your body, and make the most of it!

TAKE RESPONSIBILITY FOR YOUR BODY

Take responsibility for your body and your health. You are in control of it. It's the way it is because of your actions. It's been built by the food you eat and the lifestyle you've lived. You're running on what you ate today, not what your parents fed you when you were a baby. You're lucky to be alive at all with the body you have, and now that you have it you have to take responsibility for it.

Don't blame your genes. Sure, your parents and grandparents have a big influence on you. But you have a lot of control over your genes too. The scientific field of epigenetics proves this- you can switch genes on or off depending on what you do- if you eat good food, make good movements, or eat shit and lay on the couch. Either action will change your genes and send you deeper down that path.

You have to take responsibility right now. You may have made some mistakes or have bad momentum. Or you may be on the right track and blasting off. But either way you have to start right now with the mindset that you can make it better with what you have around you.

Taking responsibility for your body is a huge responsibility. You have to think about how to best take care of yourself. You have to nourish yourself with good food, good lifestyle, exercise, sunlight, laughter, good people, and so on. There's only 24 hours in a day for all of us and you are going to have to sacrifice and cut out some garbage to take full responsibility for your body. But it's worth it, because if you don't take responsibility for your health, don't expect anyone else to. If it's to be true it's up to you!

KNOW THE FOUR PILLARS OF HEALTH

Know the four pillars of health. If you understand and prioritize these four keys you will be on a path to enduring health, energy, mood, and efficiency. Life will become much easier and more fun. The four pillars are diet, exercise, sleep, and stress management. Prioritize these highly and you will have the leftover energy to succeed at everything else important to you.

Diet may be the most important of the four because it dictates what material your body is physically constructed from and what fuel it runs on. It's as simple as that- you are what you eat; food is fuel. Strive for a valuable vehicle that runs on premium fuel. It will be costly in some ways but will pay back tremendously in the short and long term. You don't want a cheap body. Invest in it.

The human body is meant to move. Many of our ancestors were walking a dozen miles a day for water, food, and recreation. We're not meant to sit still. We're meant to move. We have a better idea of what this means for exercise science- weight training, anatomical understanding, cardiovascular training, and so on. But you should simply be moving a lot every day and you will feel great and be doing great things for your body.

Sleep is as important as the others. At the extreme of no sleep and you will go crazy and die. Low sleep and you will develop stress disorders that wreck your body. Lots of high quality sleep will boost everything you do. Sure, you're giving up a little wakeful time but the payoff is having a better time in every hour that you're awake. Easy deal!

The last pillar of health is stress management. You can be doing everything else right but if you are stressed out all the time it can ruin your sleep which can screw up everything else. You need some strategies to put things in perspective and calm yourself down when necessary. Learn how to meditate. Take some time to give gratitude. If you can stay cool and collected in most circumstances you will be doing great things for your body.

There's complexity to good health than the four pillars, but those are the fundamentals. Still, you will have to go deeper to better understand how the body works and how to treat it just right. But prioritize diet, exercise, sleep, and stress management highly and dive deep into them and you will have a great life.

TAKE CARE OF YOUR PARTS

Take care of your parts- they are all you really have and you only get 1 of most of them. There are some exceptions to this, like if you become rich and lucky enough to replace failing parts, but for most of us we have to take care of what we have, because it's all we have.

Take care of all your parts. There are many of them, and you will have to learn about them and how to give them what they need. You have your heart, your lungs, your teeth and gums, your skin, your eyes, your various internal organs, all the joints, muscles and bones in your body, and your brain. Yes, your brain is a part. Failing to take care of your parts will make you stupider, less effective, and less successful. It will result in a worse life that doesn't last as long. You should take good care of your parts so that you can be smarter, more effective, more successful, and enjoy a higher quality of life for a longer duration. You'll be able to do better work for longer, give more love to more people, and make a bigger impact on the world. You owe it to take care of yourself.

One failing part can fuck everything up. For instance, a badly injured joint can prevent you from walking- causing your body and mind to begin to fail in other ways. Your teeth go bad and you lose them, and you're going to have a hard time feeding yourself. Gum disease is linked to heart disease. Even the way you move is linked to arthritis. It's all connected, so take care of every single piece.

Spend time, energy, and money protecting your parts. You must spend energy studying them and going about doing the things they need. You must spend time thinking about them, and how to treat them best. And you ought to spend money on them to take care of them. A healthy body is expensive! It requires expensive food, knowledge, possibly costly training, maybe premium health care. The newest procedures are only afforded by the wealthiest. This alone makes for a great reason to try and be rich. When you're wealthier it's easier to take care of your parts and live a better life for longer. But do the most with what you have for now. Take care of yourself.

GROW BIG, STRONG, AND TALL

You can grow big, strong, and tall if you want to. A lot of people will tell you it's' genetics and there's nothing you can do about it, but that's because they've given up and don't have a good understanding of the body. Sure, it's easiest when you start young, but it's never too late to start either. The body continues to grow in various ways throughout life, if it doesn't start shrinking first. Most people get shorter and shorter as they age because of shitty posture, training, and diet, and at the least this is something you can fight. But either way, growth hormones are continued to release at any age, maybe in greater quantity, maybe just a trickle, and we can grow. Or without changing the body chemistry you can stretch out the body to create space between the bones which will reduce pain and maximize length.

You probably wouldn't mind growing at least a little bigger, stronger, and taller, so you may understand this, but I'll ask- why would a man want to grow bigger, stronger, and taller? Going back to the human animal world, the male is the hunter and the combatant. He needs to go out and slay big prey- massive athletic animals and other men. When he succeeds at this he can also succeed in securing a woman and being, big, strong, and tall enough will help him protect his wife from animal threats. Things are a bit different in the modern world, but it can still be a mean physical world out there and it's good to be able to move well, be good at sports, be able to protect yourself, draw respect from men, and attract a mate. The downside is the possibility of a shorter life, and how expensive it is to be big, strong, and tall. This is a worthy tradeoff for a man. That's why we should try and get it- everyone wants it but not everyone can do it.

There is a link between the body and the brain, so growing big, strong, and tall will help you with your brainpower as well. There's some studies showing correlations between health and intelligence, height and intelligence, and so on. It will have some transfer affect. You can look at the biggest strongest athletes out there- not all of them are well educated but you can see how sharp, clear, and energetic they are- they're often as brilliant mentally as they are physically.

The first key to growing is to eat more food. Ideally the food is good quality too, or it will eventually make you sick. Back in the hunter world, only the best hunters could bring home the best game. And only the hunters bringing home the best game could eat the best food to grow stronger. It's a cycle- the stronger get stronger, the weaker get weaker, simply because of the food they eat.

The second key to growing is to train to be big, strong, and tall. Do weight training, resistance training, isometric training, postural training and stretching. And to do all this effectively you'll have to acquire a lot of knowledge.

The third key to growing is a secret for many- and that's doing things to boost your testosterone. Most men don't realize how much control we have over our T levels- it's another thing that's more in our behavior than our genetics. Some people have a lot because of the things they do, some people have very little because they neglect to act in their lives and get stuck in a rut. Once we have it we can use it to help us grow and perform better. Here's some examples of things you can do to boost your testosterone- strength training, sleeping 8+ hours of high quality sleep, winning in competition, getting sun, fasting, sprinting, having sex, just being around girls, retaining semen for a week at a time, jumping in cold water, and more. You see, you have a lot of control over everything, from the building material, to the physical pull, to the hormones.

For now, just believe you can grow bigger, stronger, and taller, seek out as much of the best food you can find, stretch (including hanging from a pull up bar), and do some basic weight training. If you did none of this you could severely stunt your growth. If you do all this you will trigger yourself to grow bigger, faster, and stronger, so you can go out and conquer other animals. But first you must conquer your own animal body.

STUDY YOUR BODY

You will have to study your body to be your healthiest and achieve the most in life. You must become knowledgeable of the workings of your body and the human body in general. If you know how it works you will understand what to do to optimize its use. If you don't study the body you won't learn enough to get great results. You will be lost, not understanding what to do, or why. You could spend a lot of time doing the wrong things and get bad results despite your hard work. But if you invest time to understand it, you will be well on your way to accomplishing your goals.

To study your body you must be curious and diligent. If you're not excited about learning to become more healthy and effective, you're doomed. But if you're excited about the idea of figuring out how it works it will be easy to take the daily action necessary to succeed. So get excited about learning how it works!

Studying your body includes reading books, watching videos, and listening to audio on body science- anatomy, biology, body mechanics, body chemistry, diet science, athletic performance, kinesiology, and on and on. You don't have to do this for your entire life but it it's worth diving deep into for a while. It will be one of the greatest long-term investments you could make. You will learn so much from people who have already done it rather than wandering around in the dark taking wrong turns. You don't have to experiment yourself much when you are regularly studying actual experiments.

Studying your body also includes paying attention to your body as you move it- how it feels as you go through regular repetitive movements, study new movements, and train. You need to understand how your joints work. Some of this you will learn from studying but some you have to learn from moving. Workout every day, learn new movements, challenge yourself, and pay attention to how your body responds.

Studying your body includes studying the foods that you eat. Your body is made of what you eat, so it's important to have a good strategy. You may not know what your optimal diet is yet, and the books will get you only partly there. You will have to introduce new foods into your diet slowly over time and see how your digestion and energy levels respond.

We will cover the important building blocks to a healthy diet in this chapter, but it won't be nearly enough to get you there on its own. You need to approach this with "If it's to be, it's up to me" and go out there thirsty to learn. Track down mentors and resources from people who are unusually healthy and you will save yourself lots of time while massively boosting your health results.

STUDY YOUR FOOD

Study your food! You are what you eat. Your body is made of foods you ate, mostly in the last year. Your body runs on the food you ate, mostly foods you ate in the last couple days. If you want to construct an awesome vehicle that runs well, you will have to have a good understanding of the food that you're eating. This requires understanding some basic diet science, studying how your body reacts to different foods, and tracking back the source of the foods that you eat. It will take some investment but it will be worth it to having the energy to tackle the important stuff in life.

Studying your food goes along with studying the body- you will have to learn some science. But a lot of it will be testing and tracking your own diet. Don't add more than 1 thing every few days if you can help it. This way you can see how your body reacts and decide if it's something you want more or less of in your diet. Over time you will be able run on a nice diverse set of foods that your body loves.

Study the source of the specific foods that you are eating. A pig is not necessarily a pig. Most pigs were processed in horrific concentrated animal feeding operations where they have little room or opportunity to express their pigness. Instead they are crammed in like prisoners, eat food they aren't supposed to eat, get no exercise or sunlight, and are shot up with hormones and antibacterials. Of course this food is going to be cancerous and cause you problems. But it's not the pig's fault! A pasture raised pig from your local farmer's market lived a totally different life and will be much more nutritious for your diet. You wouldn't know if you didn't study your food, which is why this is mandatory. You want to build your body on the best stuff so you have to know where it comes from.

LISTEN TO YOUR BODY

Listen to your body! It's smart and will be communicating with you so do your best to listen. If you don't listen to your body you can make yourself sick, weak, ineffective, and impotent. But if you listen to your body you can make yourself healthy, strong, effective, and virile! Your body will be giving you signs, so listen up.

All our head senses come through the body brain- up the nervous system, through the ancient reptilian brain, and finally up into our conscious brain. The body has communicated a lot within itself and come to a decision before you are even aware of it. At some point you will rationalize it consciously, but your body has generally decided. It's important at this point you try to trust your body and not override it. If your body wants to sleep right now, even if it's a bad time, you should do your best to take a quick nap. If you're hangry, go out and eat. It's simple. Trust your body.

Be careful though. You should be wary of the occasional wrong sense caused by evolutionary maladaptation. Our body brains are over a hundred thousand years old, but drugs and candy are brand new.

Some of us haven't had a chance to evolve out of a body reaction to eat all the sugar and take all the drugs. These are situations where you should override the body brain with the conscious mind. These are a few exceptions but very important. This is why we have a conscious mind- to catch these occasional errors.

Pay attention to your feelings and senses. Your energy level and body sensations are important, as well as your emotions. If you're feeling grumpy, you may be overloaded and need to be alone to digest information. You may be under slept. You may be dehydrated. You may be malnourished. You may be failing on your life, and that's why your body is making you feel depressed. All these so called negative emotions are important, because they will guide you to do the right thing for your body, or else you will feel shitty. But if you do the right things, you will feel good.

Occasionally there will come times where you will have to sacrifice your body and it will be necessary to override your body brain for a time. There may be a challenge you have to rise to- a once in a lifetime project with a looming deadline, trained military initiation, a championship sports game, waking from sleep to feed a child, and so on. In these cases it is a fine short term trade off to ignore the body for a while. But not as a lifestyle. Over the long run you will have to listen to and obey your body or you will pay the price. It's all you really have, and it's important that you treat it right. Your body sensations will guide you.

BALANCE YOUR BODY

A healthy body is balanced; it's relatively symmetrical. Both the left and right side are strong. The upper and lower bodies work as a unit. A body that is otherwise healthy will be prone to injury if it is unbalanced- if one side of the body is much stronger than the other or the lower and upper bodies are too separate. It's normal to be left or right handed, and imbalance will be natural, so you will have to devote some physical training to balance the body.

Most of us have tendencies towards imbalance because of our one-handedness. You are probably used to picking things up with your right hand. Which means bending down lower with the right shoulder. Doing this once or twice is not a big deal, but if you do this repetitively over a lifetime it will result in a crooked body. Unfortunately this is the norm for many people! But it's something you can fix by studying your body and training for balance.

Make a note of your asymmetrical tendencies and target those during your physical training. Your weight training is going to be symmetrical- you'll be doing the same weight on both sides of your body. And you will be doing upper / lower body combo exercises like the squat and the deadlift. But you should also be doing balancing exercises that make up for the repetitive motions you're doing outside of training. Over time you will be able to rebalance the body so everything is the same length.

The benefit will be an efficient body that feels good, has less pain, performs better, and has less injury risk. A balanced body will perform better over the long run and is worth working towards. It's up to you to balance it!

DON'T TAKE YOUR BODY FOR GRANTED

Do not take your body for granted. It's your vehicle to do and experience everything you want in life, and it won't last forever. For the vast history of the universe you did not exist, and into the endless future you will not, but for this tiny blip of time you have your body. Thank your body. It's the greatest gift you will ever receive.

Thank your body for making it this far. It may not be perfect, it may not have been treated optimally, it may be dinged up or sick, but you've made it this far. You can always try to take right action right now- to be grateful for just being able to walk if you can do that or move your big finger if that's all you have. It's still something, when it will soon be back to nothing.

Make the most of your body- not just taking care of it but making prolific and epic usage of it. Yes that includes diet and workout. But it also means adventure, discovery, journey, experimentation, and romance. You use your body for all these things.

Your body includes your brain of course. Don't take your ability to think for granted! You won't be sharp as a tack for long, so think as much as you can think right now. If you're not struck by a bus first, your youthful genius will go, and experiential wisdom will come, but that too is temporary. Make the most of your brain as much as possible as often as possible.

Your body will start to break down. It will continue to grow in some ways, but it will become damaged and diminished in other ways. Over time your hormones and chemicals will change and there will be wear and tear on the inside as well. You will grow slower and foggier. Don't take your current health for granted- maybe it could be better, but it's better now than it will be in the future. When you get injured and sick, make sure not to curse God, but to give thanks for still being able to do all the things you can still do. Don't take your body for granted! Make the most of it!

WHEN IN DOUBT, SWEAT IT OUT

When in doubt, sweat it out! If you're bored or unsure of what to do, it's always a great idea to get a little sweat going. You could go out for a fast walk, a run, some weight training, or even go into the sauna. It doesn't have to be hard necessarily. It should be enjoyable. And it will definitely feel good afterwards. Make a habit of it, and you will be sweating daily, feeling great, and performing exceptionally.

When it comes to sweating it out, find an activity that you like. It's good to try new things but it's easy if it's a routine too. What do you like to do? It could be a sport or a certain style of exercise. You do want to mix it up but having a go to will make it much easier. Over time it will become more and more routine and you will be free to revise and experiment as you go.

Don't let the difficulty of doing laundry or showering deter you from sweating. It will be worth it every time. If you have to stink for a while, or spend more money and time on laundry, it will be worth it. Those things are trivial chores in the face of a long healthy life. Anyone who doesn't want it bad enough will make excuses like this. But anyone who wants it enough will easily clear these hurdles.

The goal is to be getting a good sweat every day. This can become routine- for instance, you go for a run in the morning, or you go lift after work. But habits are also formed as a reaction to body feelings. So when your body is feeling bored, or you aren't sure what to do, go sweat it out. Just this one habit will make a tremendous difference in your health over time.

SOAK UP THE SUN

Soak up the sun. Get some nice warm sunlight on your skin. It's important for health. You can supplement with vitamin D, but it's just not the same. Most people these days are sun deficient because they spend so much time working inside. It's not optimal for health. It will leave you sick, sad, and tired. You must make it a priority to soak up some sun every day. You can get too much; you don't want to get burned. But you should try to get some every day, and if you must, go travel for it in the dark months of the year. It will boost your health and happiness tremendously.

If the sun breaks and you're inside, go out and get it. If it doesn't break all the way through, still go out and get it. Spend some time outside. Our ancestors lived outside. It's not normal to spend all hours of sunlight inside for school and work. The modern world structure sucks for sunlight, but you have some control over your own schedule and you should make the most of it by making plays for sunlight.

An important consideration for sunlight is your skin. Pigmentation is a natural sunscreen. If you are very pale you won't need as much sun. You'll burn easily. If you are very dark you will need more and may do better living closer to the equator. It's an important consideration few people make. There's a reason why traditionally pale people live in the far north and dark people live around the equator. There's a science to the skin. In the long term it will be good for you to live in a place where your natural pigmentation is optimized. But if not, you will need to vary the time you spend outside to suit your needs.

In the long run, you may want to choose a career that allows you to get sun. This doesn't mean it has to be outside work. But at the least you should be able to take control of your schedule so you can be outside when you want to be. Don't let yourself get too pale and depressed in the winter months. In the long term figure out how you can spend more time outside, and in the short term, go for the sun, because your optimal health and productivity depends on it.

HAVE FUN WITH IT

Taking great care of your body is important but that doesn't mean it has to be all serious. It should be fun! You should enjoy it. It should challenge you at times, but it can make you laugh. It can be a fun game. It can be casual. It can happen by itself

Playing sports is a great example. This is fun, but it is good strategic thinking plus tactical use of the body. It's fun and it's good for you. The options are limitless- dancing, gardening, farming, hiking, swimming, weight training, or yoga. You ought to try hard sometimes, but it doesn't have to be a grind, or unpleasant very often. It can be majority fun all the time when working out.

It's not hard to have a fun time taking care of your body because of all the endorphins that shoot off in your brain and the body changing chemicals released into your blood. "Runner's High" is the real best drug, and you don't have to run to get it! You just have to keep it moving in whatever fun way you can.

So take care of your body with love, respect the severity of the task, be grateful for this short movement to move, and have fun with it!

EAT FOR FUEL AND BUILDING MATERIAL, NOT FOR PLEASURE

When you eat food you build your body and obtain fuel to run your body. The food should taste good as a byproduct, but that is not the goal. Avoid pure mouth pleasure foods that taste great but will not build a great body or serve as good fuel. These foods may give you a quick temporary ecstasy of sugar and fat rushing into your brain, but it will not serve you in the long run. If you eat for building material and fuel, you will find that the food will still taste good, but you will feel much better over time.

Whenever you eat food, ask yourself if that food is going to be good fuel or building material. If not, try not to eat it. If it's in your hand, it may be too late. That's okay. You must attack this at the level of buying and ordering food as well. If the food isn't going to serve you outside of mouth pleasure, try to avoid buying it or ordering it. It's tempting but it's not worth it. If you must, eat before you buy food so it's not so much of a problem. If you only buy food that serves as good building material it will be much easier to eat just that food.

Over time, if you eat for mouth pleasure compared to eating for fuel and body material you will have drastically different results. The mouth pleasure route will have quick spikes of enjoyment but build a shitty low performing body that doesn't feel good. The fuel and building material method may not have the quick spikes of pleasure, but over time the body will be totally different. Your average mood will be way better and your performance on all things will be way better. You will feel better. After years of this you will be very satisfied to know what your body is made from and what it runs on. And you will have the energy to go out and crush life!

KILL FOR YOUR MEAT

Our male ancestors were hunters and warriors who journeyed out to kill for their meat. They risked their lives on long missions in the bush tracking large athletic predator animals. Along the way they might run into other armed men and must kill to survive. These men took their catch back to the tribe and shared the meat, especially with their woman and family. Together they passed down the line to us. Each of us is descended from these killer men.

Our situation is a bit different in the modern world but we still need to approach life and food with the same mentality- go out and kill for your meat. Your life depends on it. Your unborn children's lives depend on it.

You will have to venture out into the bush- into uncomfortable and sometimes unknown territory looking for opportunities. You will face enemies and obstacles along the way. They will harden you and make you grown strong and endurant. But when you see an opportunity you need to kill that opportunity. You need to treat it like you have no other choice. And when you reap the rewards you will be able to share it with who you choose.

Do whatever possible to get the best food. That hasn't changed. Our bodies are built of what we eat- it could be high fructose corn syrup or wild boar, alligator, and lion. Who do you think is going to be stronger? There's something to gaining the spirit of the animal. Farm animals are fine but go for wild fish and game when you can. Go out and break your back for the money to do it. Yes, the best food will be expensive, so kill for the money to do it. Later you will learn how to become the best at what you do so you can go out and beat out your rivals for the money trees. From this you can buy the best food- and share it!

YOU ARE WHAT YOU EAT

You are what you eat. Literally. All your cells replace themselves, generally every year. Full bone replacement might take a bit longer- more like 7 years. But most of your body is made from things that you've eaten in the last year. Most of your body in one year will be constructed of the foods you eat this year. And your body is made almost entirely of things you ate in your lifetime.

Be very, very particular about building materials for your body. You will need a lot of the good stuff to grow, but you want the highest quality material too. Cheap material leads to disease and weakness. Good material will make a better, healthier, and happier body.

Always aim for the highest quality foods to build your body out of. Everything should be sourceable if possible, at the least organic. Look for the wild stuff, the food from the pasture, from the small complex organic farms. Mass produced industrial food only when absolutely necessary, which is rare. This stuff will make you tired and sluggish and you will have to spend more energy trying to get unsick than the energy you get from the food. But if you eat only the best stuff instead you will get massive bang for your buck. You don't want a cheap body anyways. You want an expensive body, that many are envious of because few can afford. So go out and get the best building material, because you are what you eat.

EAT A VARIOUS DIET

A major key to health and performance is to eat a various diet. Eat a lot of different foods. This way you will get a variety of rare micronutrients to power your body and mind, allowing you to go out and perform. If you eat a small range of foods you may get enough protein, fat, and carbohydrates, but there is a lot more to healthy diet than just "hitting your macros". There's all sorts of vitamins and minerals that are existing in different foods and different quantities. And the more you vary your diet the more you will be able to acquire them, and the healthier you will be.

Eating a various diet starts off with being adventurous and trying new foods. Over time you will have to try a lot of new foods. You can get them by scouring the supermarket and grabbing new foods. You can get them by going to different farmers markets and trying things you haven't seen before.

When adding new foods into your diet it's important to go one at a time. Your body may or may not like the some of the things you want, and it will take a little digestion time to find out. If you try too many things at once you won't be able to isolate what is causing good or bad digestion. It generally takes about 3 days for food to totally pass through your system, so make it a basic rule to try about 1 new food every 3 days maximum. Over time you may run out of new foods to try in your area, but at that point you will be eating a nice various diet.

An easy tool for eating a rich various diet is to try to "eat the rainbow". Go for colorful food. Go for food that looks different. Go for variety of look, taste, smell, texture. This will make it more fun as well. It should be very satisfying to eat well. And when you're eating the rainbow it's going to be very enjoyable!

PRIORITIZE SLEEP

Sleep is incredibly important to good health, energy, feeling, and success. Don't listen to the people who rag on sleep- it doesn't make you lazy, it doesn't mean you don't want to be successful. A successful life should have plenty of sleep for high quality and efficient waking hours.

The research is clear on this- poor sleep (low quality or not enough) has massive negative ramifications for your body and performance. We're talking low mental clarity, low performance, bad memory, high stress, and low testosterone for muscle wasting and fat gain. Not what you want! If you get plenty of good quality sleep- 8, 9 or even more, you will feel good, perform better and more efficiently with your waking hours, and build a leaner body with higher testosterone. It's very simple but will be massively life changing.

Prioritizing sleep is a big commitment. You must come home early. You must log off early, because all those lights will suppress the sleep chemical melatonin in your brain. Cover your windows and block out any electrical lights. This will take willpower and dedication! You must make it a priority to get to bed early and sleep as much as you can to wake up naturally without an alarm. Alarms are necessary at times, especially when adjusting to new lifestyles, but if you need to be startled awake then clearly your body would have liked to sleep more. Trust your body- no alarms whenever possible. Get to bed earlier or sleep more if that's what it takes.

Sleep may be even more important than good diet and workouts. Even with those things covered, sleep poorly and you will lose it all. So put sleep up on that pedestal- some people will make fun of it, but those people aren't getting enough for themselves and usually aren't very productive in their waking hours either. The people who "don't need as much sleep" are usually wrong and not performing at their potential. Everybody needs sleep. So prioritize it!

BREATHE DEEP

Breathe deep. Breathe deep to relax. Breathe deep to calm down. Breathe deep to sleep deep. Breathe deep to take control of your stress reactions. The fourth pillar of health over diet, exercise, and sleep is stress management. How you manage your stress can be as important as anything else you're doing. If you have everything else going, but you are extremely stressed out you will release stress hormones that will reduce a lot of the good work that you've been doing. The best way to take control of yourself and stay calm is through deep breathing exercises. Do this and you'll be able to maximize your health and make it through almost anything.

Deep breathing exercises could be called meditation. It's the most effective method to take control of your nervous system. Fast, shallow breaths will speed up the heart rate into a high stress fight or flight reaction. Slow, deep breaths will slow down the heart rate into a low stress rest and digest reaction. Deep breathing is the key to taking control of these body processes.

Meditation should become a habit. It's something to do as you start planning the day. It's something you do to relax into sleep. It's something to do periodically throughout the day, and in response to stressful situations. Too many people skip this and run around in a high stress panic over things that don't matter nearly as much as they think. Deep breathing helps put you in the right frame of mind to put things in perspective- you can handle anything!

LEARN MANY MOVEMENTS

You want a body that moves well. You want an effective body. You want a smart body. You want a strong body that won't be easily injured. You want a good-looking body, but this is a bi-product of everything above. If aesthetics is the primary focus you may go down a path of repetitive movements to an injured body that looks better than it performs. Instead you want to study and learn many movements so you will be effective at a number of tasks.

You want a wide and varied movement vocabulary. Just like understanding more words helps you better understand and express your thoughts, learning more movements will help you better understand and express your spirit through your body. You will be able to do more. You will be able to try new things and be immediately good at them. You will get better at things you currently do while learning and working on new other movements.

Study more movements. Watch video tape and live athletes moving. Slow motion will help you understand. Watch different sports. Watch different activities. Watch different movements. Connect what you know with the various body sciences.

Experiment with more new movements. Make it a goal to learn 1 new move every day. This can be as simple as doing a weird movement with your body to dropping in for a lesson on a new sport. You will get a lot of mileage from trying out a lot of different things- martial arts, yoga, swimming, weight training, acrobatics, breakdance, basketball, soccer, volleyball, football, dance, and on. The more you learn the more you will be able to connect with other things you know and the more advanced you will become.

The more movements you will learn the smarter your body will be. It won't get injured nearly as easily, it will be able to do more in a day, it will feel better, and it will look better. So study up and learn as many movements as you can!

GOAL- DON'T GET INJURED

Stay healthy; don't get injured. Your body should work well all the time. If you do get injured, be smart about getting it up and running ASAP. Don't let yourself get injured; don't let yourself be a victim. You don't want any sympathy. You just want a good working body that runs well all the time.

A lot of people forget this. They train so hard they get stress fractures or tendonitis. They try so hard in sports they get reckless and tear their ankles or knees. Don't let this be you. Train hard, play hard, but train and play smart, with the simple goal of not getting injured. If a movement feels too risky, avoid it. Not every risk is worth it- especially when it comes to a good working body.

Make it a goal of your workouts and practices to not get injured. Any workout where you end both challenged and not injured should be considered a success. Any practice or game where you make it out the other side walking is a personal victory. Make it a goal and set your intention beforehand- don't get injured!

Not getting injured is a little more complicated than just setting the intention- you also have to play it tactically smart. You have to study the body and understand movements. You need to know how your joints work and how much weight they can take in various positions. You have to know how to flow energy through big impacts so even when things go wrong you end up alright. So go out and study the body so that you can stay healthy. Don't get injured!

THE FASTEST WAY TO RECOVER FROM INJURY

The fastest way to recover from injury is not what most people will tell you. There are a lot of myths on injury prevention. The science is not the popular knowledge. Most people will tell you to ice your injured body even when there is no science to support it. The most supported recovery methods are simply movement, compression, and elevation. You can walk it off. You can rub it and squeeze it to make it better. You can put your injured part up so the blood drains out of it. These are the keys.

The key is in understanding how the body works. Inflammation is not a mistake. The body wants to move as much fluid into and out of the injured area as quickly as possible. White blood cells are coming in to repair and leave. You don't want to prevent this process. You don't want to cause a traffic jam. You want to speed it up- to increase the natural inflow and outflow to the injured area.

You want to move the injured part as much as possible. Reduce, but don't over rest. Rest leads to atrophy. Lack of movement leads to pooling inflammation. Keep it moving. If all you can do is small toe or finger moves, that's what you should do. If you can do ankle or wrist circles, do that. Movement speeds the outflow. Walk as soon as you can. Get in the water as soon as you can. Move as much as you can as soon as you can.

The problem with ice is that it reduces the inflow. It prevents the repair cells from arriving on site. It's like stopping the ambulance from coming. Sure, the ambulance is going to cause a little traffic jam, but that's not a good solution. Better to do what you can to clear the traffic. Ice doesn't help clear inflammation, it just slows or delays it. Instead of icing, use movement, compression, and elevation to keep the outflow going. You will heal much faster with this method.

The proper way to heal an injured body is extremely useful to know, and it's something I wish I had told me earlier. I had many ankle sprains, bruises, bumps, and an occasional tear. For years I iced, had slow recovery, and reinjured. Eventually I was turned on to the scientific literature and realized that I was doing it all wrong. I stopped icing and started moving, massaging, and inverting more, and I was amazed out how fast I healed. I grew stronger and more protective of my joints, and the old injuries became distant memories. You don't have to learn from my pain and slow recovery. You can recover way faster with the proper strategy.

DO A LITTLE EVERY DAY

Do at least a little bit every day. It's much better to do something than nothing. And if you can consistently do something you're getting somewhere! If you think you can make it all up by going hard 1 day a week, think again. You will be in the habit of doing nothing 6 days a week which can easily turn into 7. But if you're in the habit of doing something every day, some of those days you will have the time and energy to go the extra mile.

It's very important to build the habit of doing something every day. Humans are habitual creatures.

We have automatic behaviors to repetitive triggers. We go through the motions every day. We are robotic about a lot of things. We want to use this to our advantage by setting up healthy habits to do the same productive thing every day. This way our routine becomes automatic and it's much harder to bail, and much easier to stick around to go farther. Habits are built slower than most people think, so try to work on 1 thing consistently for 2 months. Be specific about where, when, how, and why you're going to do it and you're bound to be successful.

Doing a little every day can mean a lot of things. It can mean stretching for 5 minutes every morning. It can mean running around the block in the evening. It can mean doing 20 pushups before bed. It can mean going for a walk to the grocery store every day. It could mean hanging from a pullup bar for 2 minutes a day. It could also mean reading up on the body during your lunch breaks. But so long as you take consistent action every single day, you will get there.

Doing a little every day, over time will get anything done. The great wall was laid brick by brick by brick. This book was written roughly 1 chapter a day. You may not see immediate changes but have faith that if you are consistent and persistent it will add up to big changes over time. Keep going, do a little every day, and you will be surprised by the results!

START IN THE MORNING

Start in the morning and every day will be that much easier. Your energy is sharpest in the morning. Your mind is the keenest. Your willpower is the strongest. This is the time to take care of the difficult tasks. This is the time to first challenge your body. If you can do this in the morning, the rest of the day will be relatively easy in comparison.

If you think you can wait until the evening to take care of yourself, you are in for trouble. Your energy will be low, your mind will be foggy, your discipline will be taxed. You will get it done sometimes, but other times you will phone it in, and sometimes it won't get done at all. Of course not. If you couldn't get it done in the morning when it would be easiest, how could you expect it to get done in the evening when it's hardest?

Start the day off with the most important tasks. This includes physical maintenance. You don't necessarily need to eat a great breakfast if you're doing the time restricted or intermittent fasting thing. But the morning is a great time to get moving- to walk, to stretch, to dance, to sing, to celebrate being alive in the body that you were gifted.

Study your morning routine. Start with breathing and water. Get some sunlight. Get some movement. You may not be doing all this now, but if you prioritize it you will be and soon enough it will be habit. It's worth it. With a strong start to the morning the rest of the day will take care of itself.

START IN THE EVENING

Start the next day in the evening. You want to finish strong with enough energy leftover to start working on the next day. Make plans for the next day. Eat a good dinner to energize you for the next day. Get to sleep early.

It will be hard to get a very good start to the day if you had a bad night's sleep last night. Especially if this is a consistent pattern. The easiest way to ruin your mornings is to screw up the proceeding evenings. If you do the wrong things you will set yourself up to fail. And the person to blame is yourself.

Make it easy on yourself to start the days off with a bang by doing the proper things to finish out the current day. You owe it to yourself tomorrow to take care of your business today. Feed yourself. Nourish yourself. Do the things you have to do today to end it on the best note, physically and mentally.

Study your evening routine. Make sure you're shutting off your electronics early. Make sure you're getting into bed at a reasonable hour. Make sure you've done the important tasks so you can relax and look ahead to tomorrow. Finish strong, but get started in the evening, and the mornings will be easy!

KEEP GOING THROUGH GOOD AND BAD

Keep going through good and bad! Persistence is the name of the game. So long as you get started and keep going you are gonna make it. Keeping going is the hard part. It can be easy when things are going well. But you will get hurt, you will get injured, you will get sick, you will age, your body will change over time. And you must drag yourself up and keep going every time.

If you quit, it's over. It's done. No one else is going to save you if you've given up on yourself. You won't have the energy to go out and make a good living to provide for a family, or lead a very exciting and fulfilling life. But if you just keep going, every single day, over time you will make it further and further and things will come together.

When you face setbacks you can't focus on them too much. Don't think about the bad luck, or how things used to be. Think about what actions you must take to get moving in the right direction again. This might mean combining studying the body with injury recovery. Or it might mean tweaking the diet to help recover from an illness. If you focus on these changes, good things will happen.

It's not always going to be easy. Your heart might not be in it today. You might feel sluggish. You might feel tired and old. It doesn't matter- you must keep going. It doesn't mean it has to be a grind all the time. Some days will be easier than others. But regardless of how things are going, just keep on going.

WEALTH

WEALTH AFTER HEALTH

Wealth after health. Health first, wealth second. If you have a bunch of money but your body is sick and weak, you won't have a good life. You can try to turn it around at some point, but it's better to start with the right sequence. You should be healthy as much as you can now. The healthier you are, the better a job you will do, the more money you can make, the more you can focus back on health. Do it in the right order.

Money is important, but everything has its own weight. There are a lot of people that weight money way too highly. They get rich but neglect their bodies. Even worse is how many people fail to get rich and are also unhealthy. Talk about a lose lose situation! On the other hand, there are "poor" people with healthy, happy bodies, and good relationships. Those people are still winning.

Wealth should come second after health though. It shouldn't be way down on the list. Why? Because money makes it much easier to be healthy- you can afford the good foods, you can afford the nice gyms, you can afford the adventurous outdoor excursions, you can afford good medicine if you do get sick. If you're very poor it's hard to afford the good food. So wealth comes with health, and health can come with wealth. And as your income rises you should be reinvesting into your health as the top priority.

Your track to wealth should also be a track to health. Your long-term vision for your work needs to be part of a healthy lifestyle that is conducive to a healthy body. If your track leads you to unhealthy days and a poor lifestyle, the money won't help you too much. So look far ahead down the path- you want to be wealthy, but you want that to lead you to better and better health as well.

Wealth comes after health. Not happiness or love. The reason why is some amount of wealth is necessary to keep you off the streets. You can try to be happy without a home or meaningful contribution to society, but why would you want that? You need a basic income and also meaningful work to maximize your happiness. You also need to be taking care of yourself to have good loving relationships outwardly. You can't be coming from a place of scarcity. Secure your own abundance through meaningful work and wealth acquisition, then happiness and love will come much easier.

Once you have health and wealth secured you will be much better position to be happy and enter loving relationships from actual abundance. Get these things sorted and the rest will come easily to you.

MONEY CAN BUY HAPPINESS

Money can buy happiness- to an extent. Lack of money will make you sad though. With no money to buy good food you'll have a hard time staying healthy. Without consistent money to pay rent you will be stressed with the real possibility of homelessness. You won't be able to be generous, give gifts, or make charitable donations either. There is a limit to happiness gained from money, but most people don't reach it. So while money is not the top goal, it should be a goal, because it will make it much easier to be happy.

The scientific data on this is clear. Happiness and money are correlated, up to a certain point. After that point where you're making a good living, you get diminishing returns, but not no returns. You still tend to get happier with more money, but not as much as before. The exception to this is when you're racking up millions or billions- that kind of money can be unnecessary, but still noble if you want to change the globe.

Wealth should not be the top priority, but it should be one of the top priorities. You should be healthy and you should enjoy your time. And you should have good relationships. But having a lot of

money will help in the other areas of your life. So aim
to be wealthy.

GOAL- MAKE A BIG IMPACT

Your primary goal for your work should be to
MAKE A BIG IMPACT! It should not be to make a
bunch of money or to have fun. Those things are
important, but they will come as a byproduct of making
a big impact. If you can change millions of peoples' lives
in a meaningful way you will be paid well. Wealth
comes in roughly proportional to the impact that you
put out. So make a big impact- it will be a fun challenge,
it will pay well, and it will be fulfilling.

Starting with the goal of making a lot of money
is a mistake. It's selfish and not very effective. It's
working backwards. Most extremely wealthy people
were focused on solving major problems, and that's
why they got rich. But a lot of people who make the
goal to make a lot of money end up doing things that
aren't fun, doing things that aren't in line with their
ideals, and failing to even get paid because they didn't
focus on making an impact.

When you focus on making a big impact you
will start your journey to wealth. The question is what
sort of impact you want to make? It can be specific or
general. You could focus on trying to flip an industry

on its head, or you could just try to spread a good mood. You could try to change people's lives in a very specific way. Or you could try to generally make people's lives better. Your impact can be big in scale or in scope. You can focus on reaching millions of people. Or you could focus on being a massive help to a smaller group of people. Whatever you choose, you will feel good trying, and succeed no matter what. You will also have a chance to become very wealthy!

When you have a vision to make a big helpful change, you will become very attractive. Not everyone dreams big. Not everyone actually cares to make a difference. You will attract notice. You will attract money. You will attract happiness, and you will attract love. Make it your goal to make a big impact, and over time everything will come your way.

Once you have your big impact goal, don't take too much action just yet! It's important that you study up and learn from people who have done similar things. You should start off by studying and absorbing the maximum relevant info right now. Soon enough you will be able to launch. But waiting for more information in the early stages will speed you up later.

SCHOOL IS NOT REAL LIFE

School is not real life. Being good at school doesn't necessarily translate to being good at life. Being good at school might help you, or it might even hurt you if you play the game wrong. You could rack up a huge debt investing into something you won't use later. You can be bad at school and be good at life. Or you could not even go to school and be good at life. School is optional.

It's important to understand that modern school systems are basically training you to be industrial factory laborers. They're outdated relics. It might help you be an office worker, if that's what you want. Why else would they have you sit in rows and be quiet? It's a test to see if they can plug you into the machine and you can take it. But that's not how the world works anymore. And it's never been how the world works for people who want to own the machinery.

See school for what it is- it's an opportunity to learn. Your focus should be on learning, not on grades. If you get decent grades in minimal time effort, you're winning. If you learn a lot in a little time, you're winning. If you invest way too much time in the grades and don't learn much along the way, you are losing big time.

You want to have a lot of time left over after school to work on your actual education. School will teach you only a few things, and many of them are not relevant to what you want to do in life. You need to be educating yourself with mentors, books, and jobs in your free time. You need to be training and eating healthy outside of school. So the faster and more efficient you can handle school, the further ahead you will be when you're launched into the workforce.

College is optional. If you need to go way into debt to do it, it's not worth it. It's just more of the same and you could be learning faster from YouTube videos. The loans will chain you down and limit your decision making towards jobs that will pay the loan debts. You will be restricted from experimentation, travel, and things you would rather be doing. It will suck your money, and your time.

If you're good at school, that's great, so long as you're good at other things too. You don't have to spend extra time on it. You don't have to go to college if you'd rather get started on other things first. If you're not good at school, that's ok too so long as you're good at other things. Regardless, you must be educating yourself outside of school, because school does not translate to real life, but self-education does.

READ BOOKS, SEEK MENTORS

Read books and seek mentors. Ask lots of questions. Learn as much as possible. Get as much feedback as you can. Surround yourself with people who have done or are doing the thing you want to do. Success leaves clues. Copy the winning behaviors and you will be on the fast track to success. Ignorance and solitude will confine you to the slow lane. You don't want to have to make a ton of mistakes figuring things out, and you don't have to. If you follow winners you will be able to learn from their mistakes and surpass even the greats.

Reading books is a way to tap into the greatest minds that aren't alive. You can get decades of brilliant experience condensed into a book. Download enough of this knowledge and you will be on another level. You need to access the books and you need to make time to read. Seek out libraries. They're everywhere. There are public libraries and school libraries but your friends and potential mentors will have them as well. You can begin to build your own library buying used book or on Amazon for cheap. Once you have the books you must make time for it. Set aside time in the middle of the day or make it a routine to read yourself to sleep. Whatever it is, get to reading. You won't necessarily notice a change overnight, but you will notice a massive change over time.

Seeking mentors has never been easier. It's not hard to find experts and seek them out. It's even easier to find them on YouTube or podcasts and download their knowledge. Ideally they look at what you're doing and tell you how you can do it better, but you can also follow their lead from afar. It may be worth it to get close to them if you're in their area. You may have to offer free labor or pay them for their time. But it will be worth it. Not everyone gets the privilege of professional advice and it is very valuable to your growth, so value it highly.

Almost all the most successful people are reading tons of books and learning from mentors. The richest entrepreneurs are known for how much they read. And the top people hire in the best coaches and experts to give them feedback and advice. To get to the next level you need to copy the same behaviors. It will save you massive time and energy preventing costly mistakes. And it will send you in the shortest direction towards your biggest success.

WORK FOR FUN DAYS

Work for fun days. Work can be fun. The workdays can be really fun. Work doesn't have to be a boring grind. It doesn't have to be highly stressful. It can be enriching, soothing, and nourishing. Having fun days is a fine goal for work. It is a good criterion for selecting a job, career, business, or employer. They say if you love what you do, you never work a day in your life. If you have a fun time working, you will have a fun life. That joy will bleed out into everything else you're doing and those around you will be thankful for it.

What's fun will mean different things to different people but there are some fundamentals to it. It's fun to use your brain. It's fun to use your body. It's fun to try new things. It's fun to master things. It's fun to work with a team. It's fun to accomplish goals and tasks. Beyond this, the playground is wide open. Look for opportunities to carve out a more fun space, whether it is more creative problem solving, more outdoor work, a more fun team, or whatever it is that gets you going.

When it comes to seeking fun there are two approaches- going to the fun or building more fun around you. If you aren't having a lot of fun with your job, it could mean it's time to go looking for something else. Or it could mean you should be investing more energy into making your current job more fun. You could try cracking more jokes or throwing out more ideas. You can give everyone more thanks and appreciation and watch the organization change. It's possible you can take what you already have and make it way better.

A lot of people don't think work can be fun. They spent their lives glued to a desk or doing something else they don't really enjoy that much, because they think it's the best they can do. It shouldn't necessarily be fun, but it can be. You can have a lot of fun with your work, if you try. Try to have more fun with your work and it will make a massive difference to your happiness.

THE 4 HOUR WORKWEEK IS REAL (BUT BORING)

It's possible to have a passive income money tree that allows you to work only 4 hours a week... but it turns out it's boring. It's more fun to have work you enjoy, that makes a difference, that is fulfilling. The idea of having a vacation lifestyle is a cool idea, but it gets old fast. The reason why is because as humans we are extremely social animals and work plays an important part of our social connections and societal belonging. We feel our best when we are an important part of teams and communities. When you're not working, everyone else is still working, and you will get bored. So don't make it a goal. A better goal is to find some work you love. Or if you are lucky enough to figure out how to get passive income going, use that to go pursue the job you love.

I will tell you that this is real from experience. I read Tim Ferriss' "The Four-Hour Workweek" when I was young and I dreamed of doing it myself. Eventually I did- I optimized my blog to minimize the hours, and eventually launched a coaching business that mostly ran itself. I used the money and time to travel the world and try out a variety of lifestyles- online content productions, basketball player, surfer, and so on. It got old fast. I realized that if I wanted a fun life with good social connections I should recommit to working. I used my passive income to become an organic farmer in Hawaii and I'm much happier to do 40 hours of manual labor a week than to have no commitments at all. But I could have skipped the pursuit of vacation to start organic farming a decade earlier and probably would have been much happier.

Go straight for the job or work you like. You will have to experiment some to get there, but don't go into it with an outcome dependence. Don't hope for big money with no work. You may fail to hit the numbers and you might like your work either. I am a special case- I got lucky. Most people who try to do that fail or get trapped in an endless grind. And even when I succeeded I realized it wasn't how I wanted to be spending my time anyways.

Life is better with commitments. Commitments to yourself, commitments to your relationships, and commitments to work. This is the social cement that connects us to other people. An idle life is not a good life. Not working gets boring fast. Work is fun. Shoot for work that you love.

BUILD A HELPFUL SYSTEM

Build a helpful system. That should be your goal if you want to own a business. Build a system that takes someone from a pain point or need and and brings them out healed and stronger on the other end. Make it as systematic as possible- plug in automation and delegation wherever you can so that you can step back as the creator for the system and let the cogs of helpfulness turn. This is how you create a 4-hour workweek. This is how you create passive impact (and passive income). And this will free you up to do the work you want, to provide for who you want, to spend your time how you want.

It won't be easy to build a helpful system that runs itself, but it's possible. It will take both hard work and smart work. You will have to look at many other similar business models. You will have to spend some money. You will have to read books, listen to YouTube, and seek feedback from mentors. You will have to run experiments and tests. But if you do all these things for long enough, you will create an epic system of helpfulness and everyone will win.

You will have to see the system to truly understand it. Draw it on paper. Look at all the actions. Look at the funnel. Look at where prospects enter and clients exit. Look at how the system will change people. Look at all the various steps of commitment and delivery along the way. For each of these small operations, look to automate and delegate whenever possible, or whenever you aren't extremely passionate about the work. See if a robot can do it. If not, train a human to do it. Your time is most important spent building the system, maintaining it, and doing passionate work.

A systems building mindset is extremely altruistic and you will be rewarded heavily for it. If you remove yourself from the equation you can focus on others. You need humility enough to relinquish control over everything. To focus on improving other people's lives even when you sleep. And it will free up your own time to do yet more work, if that's what you choose. It will also allow you to spend more time adventuring, traveling, exploring, working on your health, spending time with your family, or whatever you choose. It's worth it to build a helpful system.

MONEY TREES ARE REAL

Just like 4-hour work weeks are real, money trees are real. Money trees are seeds that you plant, seedlings that you water, that eventually bear fruit. They can eventually produce fruit season after season with little upkeep. But if you don't take care of them they will wither. Eventually they will die. But it's possible to have a money tree to allow you to travel, adventure, work on health, spend time on relationships, or do whatever work you really want to do.

Money trees take a few forms. One form is the online business system. If a business system helps people, changes their lives, makes their situation better, it doesn't matter that it's all automated. Nobody cares that you are doing whatever you want- in fact it's better marketing. An online business that is well delegated can produce fruit for years and open many doors for you. This is perhaps the most rewarding because it comes with the knowledge that you're delivering value and making a difference.

Another common form of a money tree is a rental property. If you delegate out the management, eventually all you will have to do is collect monthly rent checks. There are other investment opportunities like this. But none of them will develop purely by chance.

You will have to put conscious thought into making a money tree fruit for you.

The conventional hourly or salary job is selfish. You are expecting to get paid for your time, as opposed to getting paid for making a difference. The goal of a money tree is to untether your time from your money. Your money should be tethered to your impact. Make a big impact with a little time and you have a money tree. Keep watering it and it will keep bearing fruit for you.

THROUGH RAIN, SLEET, AND SNOW

You must keep going, through rain, sleet, and snow. Keep going under any conditions. Don't give up over any circumstances. Most people will take a day off when they feel sick. A day turns into a week. Momentum is gone. Nothing is done. Meanwhile if you just keep grinding it out, every single day, no matter how you feel, you will get there. Persistence is the key to success, and you must persist through all weathers.

Persisting through rain, sleet, and snow doesn't mean it's going to be dark and cold all the time. Most of the time it can be good. Ideally most of the days are good. But not every part of a day is good. Not every full day is good. Sometimes it dumps on you. And if you can keep going until the sun comes back out, it will become easy again. You will be that much further ahead of the competition just for that.

The most successful people keep working. Some of them work 7 days a week. It's easy when they love what they're doing and believe in the vision they're working towards. Life is going to throw some inconvenience at you, and the best people keep on going regardless. If you can be as persistent as the best, you will eventually become the best.

HOLD THE SPACE

If you build it, they will come, but only if you hold the space. If they show up and no one is there to let them in, they won't come back. You must be in the habit of being there every single time, no matter what. To do a good job, you must hold the space at your job. To launch a new business, you have to hold the space in your business. To hold a new weekly meeting, you have to be there every single week. Most people can't build it in the first place. Most aren't consistent enough to keep it going after that. They break momentum. If you can just be there every single time, no matter how you are feeling, what you've built will become bigger and bigger.

Be extremely reliable. You don't have to feel good all the time, but you must be there every time. If you're trying to be a YouTuber, you can't miss a day, even if you were busy. If you are trying to be a coach, you can't miss a coaching call. It's really that simple. But it's hard, because this reliability is built on wealth.

If you don't put health before wealth, you will struggle to hold the space because you won't always have the energy. You'll make yourself sick and have to cancel. You'll work yourself into unemployment and bankruptcy. But if you build in a foundation of health it will be easy to show up every time. You'll have the energy to make it through rain, sleet, or snow. And you will continue to build momentum.

Be consistent, be reliable. Don't start something if you aren't prepared to hold the space. If no one shows, no one knows. Hold the space again next week, because if one person showed up and you weren't there, they won't be back. Success is built on small gains and individual relationships. Be there to hold it down and it will grow.

LOVE WHAT YOU DO

You should love what you do. But you don't necessarily have to "do what you love". Doing what you love may not pay well if it it's idle and not helpful to other people. If you love helping people, then sure, do what you love. But otherwise, you need to find a way to love what you do.

Look on the bright side of things. Recognize that you have an opportunity to make a difference. Even if it seems small, you can make ripples through society. Say that you are a food service person like a barista. It may seem like you don't have a ton of leverage to make a big impact, and to an extent that's true. But if you find a way to love what you do you will go the extra mile to make a difference. You can change people's days as you interact with them, and by brightening their moods you will help them go out and do a better job of what they're doing. The butterfly effect could brighten a lot of people's days. It's possible to make a huge difference with the right attitude.

What career you choose is somewhat arbitrary. Sure, some jobs may be a better fit than others. Some careers lead to a great healthy lifestyle, others don't. But beyond that, it's almost all the same. There's thousands of careers and we must commit to something at some point. But whatever that career is a vessel to make a big impact. If your goal is to spread joy, you can do that with literally any job. It doesn't matter. What matters is your approach- loving what you do.

You should find a way to love what you do because we don't have that much time here on this

Earth. It's a massive waste of your most precious resource to not love what you do. If you must quit your job and do something else, then sure. But it may be as simple as just accepting your position and injecting as much love into your work as you can right now. If you only have 1 shot at life, it's way worth it to do what you love.

FEEDBACK BEATS PRAISE

Seek out feedback, not praise. Praise may feel good, but it's not particularly helpful- you already know if you did a good job. On the other hand, feedback may be painful, but it's extremely helpful- you don't always know you did a poor job, and you won't know why. It's extremely valuable to have an expert point out all your mistakes, even if it can be a bit painful. The key to this is swallowing your pride and humbling yourself. Attention is valuable, and if someone with experience is willing to spend time looking at what your doing, treat that as gold.

Most people seek praise instead of feedback because they can't handle the truth. Most people are not humble enough to get better. They would rather stay bad than learn why they're bad. The good news is if you seek feedback instead of praise, you are not like most people. You will be special and will be able to advance way faster than the average person.

The keys to getting feedback are seeking it and asking it. You must go beyond accepting it and actively search for it. Get in the same room as people who do what you want to do. Ask people to look at what you're doing. Post your work on the internet and welcome criticism.

You may have been told to ignore haters, but this is often bad advice. Unqualified feedback from scrubs will not help you, so you should screen that out. But you should welcome the criticism of people who are legitimately experienced. They're not hating on you- they're just pointing out what you're doing wrong. They may even hate your technique, but you are more than your technique. You have room to grow and seeking feedback is a great way to do it.

The people who ignore feedback and seek praise tend to get stuck in the mud. They don't advance and they don't realize they aren't getting better because they screen out any help that comes their way. By simply recognizing harsh feedback as being helpful, listening to it, and implementing it, you will grow and learn extremely fast. You will become good at what you do, and doors will open for you.

BE GOOD AT A FEW THINGS

Be good at a few things. Try to be great at one thing. Be decent at a lot of things. But you can be mediocre or downright bad at everything else, and it's okay. Humans are meant to specialize. You don't have to shore up every weakness. You can be a jack of many trades, but you shouldn't try to be a jack of all trades. You should try to get good at a couple things, and that will take you incredibly far towards success.

Most successful people are truly great at only one thing. They hit one home run in business. They became a professional at one thing. That's good enough. You don't want to be bad at health, happiness, and love, so those are a few of the other things you can should strive to be good at. But beyond that you shouldn't try to learn everything about everything. You should try to learn a lot about one thing and at most a little about everything else. You will stand out for being exceptional at what you do, and no one will care that you aren't good at the infinite other things that you don't do.

It's okay to have weaknesses so long as you have a strength. If you are extremely good at one thing, it will make up for almost everything else. If you are very good at a few things, you will have the option to combine skills. Beyond that, there just isn't enough time to be great at everything, and it shouldn't be a goal. Aim to be good and you will become great.

PLAY FOR THE BEST POSSIBLE SCENARIO

Play for the best possible scenario. Shoot for the maximum possible upside. Think about what is the best case and go for that. You only have 1 chance at this with this body and this life. Do not waste this opportunity. Life is too short to not go for it. But it's also too long to live a boring life. So think about what you want in life and make a play for it!

The first step is figuring out what you want to do. Some people know early. But a lot of people don't have this figured out yet. And you can't blame them, because they haven't tried very many things. How can you know what you want to do with your life if you haven't done anything? So you must start off with experimentation. You might have an idea of what you want to do, but you don't want to get married to it before you try it. Put in the effort to experiment, try different jobs, learn different fields, travel, and see what's possible. You might fall in love with something you totally didn't expect, and you would never have found out if you hadn't been experimenting.

Once you know what you want, it's up to you to pursue it every single day. You can't take a day off your life when you're working for your life. If you want to write, write every day. If you want to be an athlete, train every day. If you want to make a difference, study every day. We are creatures of habit and the daily experimentation and revision will slowly get you there.

Some people will tell you to play it safe. They might care about you and might think they have your best interested in mind. But they're scared to see you fail. They were scared to fail themselves and never went for it. You must ignore these people for the time being- they will understand later. You can appease them somewhat by making a play for security while you work towards your dream- taking two jobs for example. This may be necessary to stay afloat, but it might just take time away from what you really want to be doing and slow you down.

When it comes to obtaining the good life of your dreams, you must pursue what you want. If you make too many concessions for safety and convenience you will get stuck in a life that is merely okay. Merely okay is just not good enough for your only chance at this. You don't have a bunch of lives to restart in this body. You only have 1. So shoot high and keep shooting high. It will be worth it.

TAKING NO RISK IS A GUARANTEED LOSS

Taking no risk is a guaranteed loss. This is especially true of men. Men are born in higher numbers. There are about 5 extra men per 100 women. There is a surplus of tens of millions of men in their 20s and 30s. You can check the world census by age to confirm this. What this means is, as a man, if you play it safe in your room, no one will come looking for you. No one will notice you're missing. No one will knock on your door to find you feeling sorry for yourself. By taking no risks you will make yourself invisible and lose by default.

There's a reason why men take so much dangerous risk- wars, construction, or just driving fast. It's in our blood. We must. We need to get an edge over the competition somehow. Play for high variance. If you lose, you would have lost anyway. But if you win, you win big. You win health, you win money, you win love, you win happiness.

Play for your dreams. Adventure and travel. Take a shot at things. Go for it even when the odds aren't great. Taking no risk automatically sends you to conventional results. Playing things safe and taking the secure jobs may lead to a living more of the time, but it is a mediocre living. We're looking to make a killing and live our optimal life. To hit a home run we need to spin the dice sometimes and go for it!

STUDY YOUR MARKET

Study your market. You have to know what's going on. To dominate a market you need to know who's in the market, the size of the market, the various buyers and sellers, the professionals, the strategies, and more. It won't be easy, but that means most people won't be doing it so it will be easy to get ahead. Go above and beyond to educate yourself about what you're doing and how it relates to other things. Many people don't take the extra time, but you can and it will pay off for you.

You have to know your market, but don't confuse that with knowing everything about other markets. It helps to have other systems to draw from but you can't try to learn everything, it's just too much. It's fine to narrow it down so you can get more in depth. There aren't many dedicated specialists, so it pays to be a specialist. Put in the time. It's worth it.

Look at your market from as many angles as you can. The professional. The amateur. The vendor. The fan. The software. The social media. The accounting. The history. The new trends. The next big thing. It will all come together. You can see the matrix. You will be able to use the information to dominate the market from your own winning angle.

Draw from a variety of resources. Social media. Message boards. Print. Events and conventions. Seek out the top dogs and try to learn from them. Most people won't get the extra mile to get this level of information. Sure, it will take a good amount of time, but the efficiencies uncovered will grow and accelerate later to blast off.

STAY IN YOUR LANE

Stay in your lane. Know what you're good at and stick with that. Teach only what you know. Focus on your specialty. Go deeper into the space, rather than trying to do everything. If you try to do too much you will be poor at everything. If you try to teach what you don't know you will fail. If you speak out on things you aren't an expert on you will be humbled. Whether you are an entrepreneur or not, you are your own brand of business. Protect your brand by staying in your lane. A few mistakes can cost you badly. You can bounce back, but you don't have to. It's better to keep going up and up and up.

Staying in your lane takes humility. It requires you knowing what you're good and bad at. It requires holding your tongue when you know a little bit about something. It requires asking more questions rather than parroting off what you've learned. Many people never learn this. Some have to go through extreme trauma to learn this. You don't have to. This is a lesson you should learn early and save yourself the painful mistakes of being too vocal about things you know little about and trying to sell services you are mediocre at best at. The upside of staying in your lane is more about avoiding catastrophic pain than rich rewards. But it's avoiding the setbacks that will get you to the rich rewards that much sooner. Be humble and stay in your lane. You'll get there.

WORK FOR FREE

Contrary to what most people will tell you, you should start out working for free. And you should continue to work for free, even after people are paying you. Work first, maybe get paid later. The more value you create, the more you will get paid later. If you are always waiting to get paid before doing anything, you won't do nearly as much and you won't get paid nearly as much in the long term.

Unpaid internships are great opportunities. Humans have been doing apprenticeships for many thousands of years. You work for free, in exchange they teach you some things. Why would you expect to get paid when you are a beginner anyways? As a rookie you have very little value to offer so you shouldn't expect much compensation. You should expect to put as much work as possible until you have the veteran skills to command a good pay. But to do that you will have to work for free, seek feedback, get mentorship, and keep going.

Working for free extends way beyond unpaid internship type deals. Writing a book, like this for example, usually requires working for free- possibly for many hours, weeks, months, or even years. Maybe far down the line you will get paid, maybe not. But if you're waiting for a book deal before you get started, forget it, it's unlikely to ever happen.

Working for free is also necessary to start a business. You should have a value ladder and a sales funnel. But the upfront should always be free. The YouTube is free, the social media is free. There should be free ebooks and products. The more you give for free, the more you might receive later. This is the reciprocity effect in action. Humans are very reciprocal. If you help them, they will often help you back. So you should be making a lot of free offers when you're starting, and even when you're established.

It's counter intuitive that working for free would lead to higher pay, but that's how it goes. Focus on making a big difference and working for free for now. As the scope of your impact increases and you help more people, you will be rewarded. But if you keep waiting for money before you get started, you probably won't ever get started. So even if you have no offer, and especially if you have no money, get started right now working for free.

EXPERIMENT

The more experiments you can run, the more you will learn, the faster you will advance, the more success you will find. If you're doing a good job of asking, learning, and seeking feedback from mentors you won't have to run every experiment- many of them are done for you, and you don't have to repeat them. But not every experiment can be run for your life, and you will have to try many approaches to many things.

There are a variety of experiments to run. One of them is on what sort of work and career you want to do for the long haul. You may have an early idea, but you could be wrong. You might not have an idea, and you have to find out. The best way is to try lots of things. Put yourself out there. Take unusual jobs. You will find out quickly what you don't like and might be surprised at what you like the most. Not everyone does this and many people get locked into work they hate. So make sure to run experiments for work before you make any long-term commitment.

As you narrow down your mission and work, you will want to revise your approach through experimentation. Try new methods of doing things. Make new suggestions. Throw out new products. If it doesn't work the first time, that's ok, it was an experiment. Experiments are not meant to make everything work right away- they're meant to give you more information about what may not work. If you stick to the same approach because you are afraid to fail, you are guaranteed to fail because you will be slow to adapt. But if you are willing to spend some time to run some experiments, you will eventually find a much better approach and leapfrog everyone who had a head start.

It's important to track your experiments whenever possible. Experiments should be scientific, with careful tracking. If you don't track anything, you can't know for sure how it worked. But if you have numbers to back it up you will quickly learn which approach works better. It takes extra time to track, but it is worth it. Over time you will learn more and more, where in another reality you tried one thing and stuck with it forever.

Running experiments is the key to learning the best methods. You don't have to run every experiment.

You should avoid running very costly experiments. You should learn from others whenever possible. But you will have to run experiments for your own life and approach to discover the best methods for you.

PLAY FOR A GOOD TEAM

Play for a good team. Play for a high performing company or organization. Get good people around you. Surround yourself with high performers. Learn from practitioners. Don't try to do it on your own, and don't play for a bad team. Doing it on your own will leave you trying to reinvent the wheel by yourself. You will make way too many mistakes and probably won't succeed. Playing for a bad team will teach you how to lose. It will engrain bad habits. Seek out the good teams and play for them.

The quality of the team should always be an important consideration with the work. Even if you love the work, if you hate the team you will have problems. In that case you're signing up for the short term. A great team will make the work fun. It's infectious. You will raise each other up. You will accomplish more than you would have otherwise. You will be energized to go home and grind on your own projects. You will learn faster and level up quicker.

Even if you are starting off your own business, you should still play for a good team. First, make sure you have learned from practitioners before you do your own thing. And as you do your own thing make it your first step to do our own thing. Bring in good people. Spend your time partnering and hiring. Human resources are your most valuable resources. If you build a good team your business or project will take off, with or without you.

BE THE HARDEST WORKER

If you work harder than anyone else, you're bound to surpass everyone else. There are a few other variables; you must work smart and avoid too many costly mistakes. It's possible to work very hard but be very inefficient and ineffective. That's rare though. Most of the time hard work will get you there, because hard work includes more than putting in the hours. It means taking the work seriously enough to study it, to study the process, to study yourself as you do the work. If you work hard, you will challenge those around you to work hard, and you will be able to select hard workers for your circle.

One of the keys to hard work is showing up early and leaving late. Working Friday nights and weekends. You don't have to do this for no thanks and no pay.

And it doesn't have to be a grind all the time either. It can be fun. The extra hours you put into work can be put into your body, put into your knowledge base, put into researching your market, put into your clientele, or just put into what you think is both fun and productive. If you work these hours though you will be very satisfied to know that you are outworking everyone else and you are bound to succeed for this.

Almost all the most successful people were extremely hard workers. Many of them were extremely smart workers as well. But all of them were putting in the extra hours, going the extra mile, for months, years, decades, a lifetime. If you follow their work ethic, you will inspire and you will succeed.

MAKE AN OFFER

Make an offer. Make sure they are the right fit and let them know how you can help them. Then ask them to sign up. Ask them to sign here. Ask them to make a commitment. Ask them to send over a deposit. Ask them to sign up for a recurring plan. If it's scary, you will have to do it anyways. You need to make sales. Everything is sales. Getting a job is sales. You must boldly put yourself out there. You don't want a million rejections, but there are plenty of fish in the sea. If they aren't down, you don't have to convince them, just go looking for the next lead. But if you procrastinate making an offer you will waste too much time. Make an offer so you can move on to someone who wants you. This way you can spend more of your time in service if that's what you want. You will also make more money, gain more clients, and make a bigger impact.

There are incredible performers who never get paid because they never make offers. Artists still need to sell their art. Everyone needs to get paid for their work. If you can't negotiate you are in trouble. You will stay poor. It helps a lot to be exceptional. You want to be so good they can't ignore you. But other people don't have your best interest like you have your best interest. You can't rely on other people to make the best offers for you. You must sell yourself. Find leads, make offers, serve those who want to be served, and move on. It's a simple wealth equation. Now go put yourself out there!

MAKE THEM COME TO YOU

As you level up in work you will have more ability to make them come to you. You can make your ideal customers come to you. You can make your ideal employees or employers come to you. You can be headhunted and highly sought after. This is much more enjoyable and sustainable than cold calling and knocking door to door. When they come to you, you will have to spend less energy on selling, interviewing, and applying and more time to deliver, master your skills, and do everything else.

The alternative to making them come to you is always going out and seeking. Outbound calls, outbound meetings, cold calls, door to door, etc. It's a lot of energy for not a lot of return, because these people are not seeking you. They aren't warm to your idea. They don't know you so they don't trust you. You don't need a yes from everyone, and you don't need to make it that hard on yourself. Instead identify the people who are actively seeking you and find a way to let them find you. You'll instead have inbound calls and inbound meetings. Possibly so many that you can't handle it all and get to pick and choose exactly who you work with.

The first key to making them come to you is being so good they can't ignore you. If you are a leader in the field doing extraordinary work you will attract notice and attention. If you are still a beginner, attention won't be nearly as helpful anyways, because you won't be ready to work with the best. As you become better over time this will happen naturally. You'll become better connected, make more news, and become highly sought after.

Once you are extremely good at what you do, it's time to amplify your attention. You will be attracting much of it naturally, but it helps to have a marketing plan to get more eyes. Word of mouth testimonials can do a lot for you, but the potential for epic viewership is attainable. Print ads are dead, and specially targeted internet advertising has become cheap and affordable for everyone. You can run targeted ads to your ideal clients, to your ideal employers, to your ideal employees. Assuming you are approaching mastery you will know how to handle all this attention and connections and will be able to blast off from it.

ACCEPT 'NOS' AND MOVE ON QUICKLY

You don't need to convince everyone that your dream is achievable. You don't need to convince everyone your product or service is good for them. You don't need to have everyone like you. There are many fish in the sea and you should not waste time trying to catch the elusive ones. You can learn a little from them but let them go. Don't try to convince them. It's not right. Spend your extra time on the people who are giving you yes. These people will stick around for the long haul and you will be better for it.

There's some mythology that you shouldn't take no for an answer. That you must convince everyone that you're right. This is false. It's a huge waste of time. You aren't likely to convince everyone who already has their mind made up. Not everyone is going to like you. It's not a big deal. But some people will, and if you get enough of them and continue to serve them, you will have your own business and gain control to do a lot of things that you want.

LEVERAGE YOUR RESOURCES

Leverage your resources. Make the most of everything extra you have. Maximize your money, your connections, your equipment, your skill. Leverage lets small weight go a long way. If you place 20 pounds right on a teeter totter it can lift 100 pounds. But 100 pounds placed wrong can't even lift 20. This is about working smart, not just hard. Put things in the right place and a small bit of work will go a long way. Leverage can work exponentially and is the key to blasting off and staying up.

Leverage is all about making the most of what you have and not wasting anything. If you have extra cash in the bank it can be put to work for you. Instead of saving a pool of money for later you can leverage it to earn you money back via financial investment, certification, ads, new equipment and so on. If you have certifications, use them. If you have equipment, use it. If you can make use of ads, leverage your money to get a million eyes on your work.

Leverage has a multiplicative effect to boost end results. Ads can be the lever to multiply your impact. Social media can be the lever to multiply your voice. Money can be the lever to multiply your ads. Certifications can be the lever to multiply your authority. If you let everything stay separate and stagnant, nothing will happen. You have to see the teeter totter and place things just right to use what you have to multiply your results.

Two people can have the same resources and put in the same amount of time and get dramatically different results. One person uses what they have to make exponential gains, the other person doesn't make much use of what they have and has to keep on grinding. Be smart about your work, especially with the resources that you can control. Always look to multiply and 10x what you have. It will make a huge difference in your success equation.

LEARN TO DELEGATE

Learn to delegate. Learn to partner. Form teams. Get other people to do the things you aren't good at. Focus only on the things you are best at. There's not enough time in the day to do everything, and you don't have to. If you try to do everything yourself you will either fail or work massive hours for meager return. You only have to do the few most important things. Let your team do the rest for you.

Learning to delegate starts with self-awareness and humility. Some people can't delegate and become control freaks because they aren't aware enough to realize that they need to stay in their lane and let other people do their thing. It's humbling but you must identify what you are truly not good at and what you aren't capable of doing. Those are the places to delegate and partner around.

You should always be thinking about tasks that you can delegate and outsource. What is consuming a lot of time? What are you doing that really sucks? What tasks are boring? What areas aren't getting you results? These are all opportunities to benefit from delegating.

Once you figure out what to delegate you have to find the right people and motivate them. The ideal candidate comes to you and makes an offer, but you can also find them through social media postings or online job boards like Upwork. You'll want to test out a few candidates for any job ideally, because not everyone will follow through and it's much easier to fire someone before they get started so you don't have to later. When it comes to motivation money will be a factor but there's a lot more than that. We don't do everything for money. A lot of people just want recognition, want work trade, or want to be part of something. If you let them have that, they will work for you. But even if you pay them the best, if you treat them like shit they will leave and you will be left on your own. Reward your team for doing the work you can't.

As you master delegation you will free up more and more time to focus on a few things you truly want. This will allow you to have more fun and to truly master things. Mastery takes many hours, and that means not trying to do everything. It will also allow the possibility of a 4-hour workweek or money tree business. It will give you more time to focus back on your health and spend with loved ones. Learn to delegate, it will be worth it!

BE A GOOD LEADER AND MANAGER

You have to be a good leader and manager in order to build great things. Great projects and businesses have great leaders. Great teams have great managers. If you can't lead and manage well, everything you try to build will crumble. Your people will leave and you will spend costly time retraining and replacing them. Customers will follow suit. You have to keep your people and in order to do that you must be a good leader and manager.

To be a good leader must have a good vision and be a good example. Let your team know that it's about more than making money- the work you're doing is important. Share with them the full vision, the emotions behind it, and why it matters. Then lead them with example. Put in more hours than everyone else. Do a better job. Be extremely reliable. Set a high bar for yourself and your team will be inspired to follow.

To be a good manager you have to give ownership to your team. This is really important and often neglected. Don't micro manage them. Give them some room to do their own thing. If they understand the vision they will know what they're doing. Trust them to be autonomous and verify them only occasionally. Let them know they're doing good work. Thank them for their contribution. It goes way beyond this though.

A massive key to good leadership and management is to give your team the keys to raise themselves up. Don't be the obstacle between them and making more impact and money. Don't force them to negotiate for a raise with you to get paid more. Give them opportunities to increase their own responsibility and pay. Let them work for commission. Give them tools for interdependent entrepreneurship. Let them create their own vision for their own future working with you. They will be inspired by this and want to stick around for the long haul. They will do so much more alone than if you limited their control and pay.

And you will do so much more together as a team than you could have done alone.

LEARN TO AUTOMATE

Learning to automate will massively free up your time to do what you want. Harnessing automation is like delegating, except you are using computer and internet tools to work for you instead of people. Automation tends to be much cheaper and simpler- but it can also be much more reliable! Think about it. You shouldn't have to spend time on repetitive internet tasks like posting content between platforms, copying down payments for your accounting, sending emails triggered off payments, and so on. You can use internet tools for this saving you time to do what you want.

A basic example of automation is any social media post, such as YouTube. Sure, you spent the time to post it. But now you have this robot version of you up that will play whenever anyone clicks in. While you're sleeping, someone will be learning from you. Compared with going around and talking to people 1 on by, the automated video version of you is making a massive difference. It's magical, and a tool that should not be wasted.

A more complex version of automation is having a sign-up form that triggers a series of prewritten emails. Something like this is a massive time saver. You write the emails one time, and they can send out for years. For tools like this in 2018 I recommend Zapier especially.

Your approach to automation should be all about spending a little bit of time now to free up more time later. To be sure, you want good days today. But it's fine to sacrifice an hour here and there to free up 10 hours later. It makes sense. Any sort of repetitive task should be automated immediately. This is the highest priority. It should not be put off, because the earlier you do it, the more time you will save to do the things you want- like work on your health, the work you want, relationships, and so on.

UNCHAIN YOUR MONEY FROM TIME

Forget the notion that you should be paid for your time. That's selfish. It's also unmotivating. Anyone can clock the hours, but not everyone can make the impact. Impact should be more closely related with pay. If you make a massive impact, you ought to be paid well, whether you spent a little time or a lot of time. Think if you are an automobile. You shouldn't be paid more for taking a longer time to reach your destination.

You should be paid less. You should be paid more for doing it better and faster.

The good news about untethering time and pay is you can drastically increase your income. If you are working hourly or salary you are severely capped. But if you are working for impact, it becomes unlimited. This is how millionaires and billionaires are made- not from working infinite hours, but from untethering time and money and making a big impact.

If you help someone transform their life you ought to be paid well, even if you spent the time two years ago setting up a system that you are just maintaining now. Automation is a tool to reach a bigger audience and you ought to be paid more for it. Delegation is a way to make a bigger impact and your team should be paid more for it. The more products you sell, the more you will be paid. It has very little to do with time. It has everything to do with efficiency and impact.

Rethink your financial goals around making the largest impact. Forget salary and hourly. You will be paid more, do more, affect more, have more, and spend less time. It's possible.

SAVE TIME LATER RIGHT NOW

You should be automating and delegating as much as you can, right now, like right this second. The reason is automating repetitive tasks will save you more time the sooner you do it. You should be trying to enjoy your days but if you could spend 10 minutes today to save 1 minute every day for the next year you will soon return your investment and save hours on the year. Any opportunity to save hours like this is an incredible investment, and the best time to act on these is today. If you make this a priority you will free up tons of time, allowing you to pursue what you want to pursue.

We've already talked about automation and delegation so we'll focus on the mindset of saving time for later right now. The math of saving the time makes sense, but that' doesn't make it easy. It requires some delayed gratification. It requires doing an annoying task right now when you would rather be doing something else. It steals time from you in the short term, which means many people can't make this happen. But if you can see ahead and are willing to put in a small sacrifice, it will begin to pay off big time over the long time.

Life is short and tomorrow is not promised. But tomorrow is likely. You don't know that you will live more years, but you probably will. It may not be worth it to make major sacrifices for decades long return, because that is much less certain. But if you are getting majorly paid back in months or years, it will be worth it to give something up now. It would be a good investment with money, and an even better investment of time. You will probably live quite a bit longer, and you want to have better control of your time in that future, so make plays for it.

INVEST IN CASH FLOW

Financial wealth could imply holdings or cash flow. Holdings being liquid cash and investments, cash flow being what's coming in every day or month. It's nice to have holdings. It will reduce anxiety. But if you have holdings and no cash flow, those holding will eventually run out and you'll be budgeting and projecting the whole way. At the other extreme, you could have no holdings but massive cash flow and you know you'll be good. Cash flow is a major anxiety reducer. It will pay the bills in the short term and the long term. Cash flow is something to strive for, and it's something to invest in to create a money system to free you up to do what you really want to do.

Investing in cash flow is about spending time, energy, and/or money to set up a recurring cash flow back to you over time. Perhaps the most common example of this is having rental property. You spend money up front on your house and will collect a steady monthly cash flow as long as you can keep your tenants managed. In this case you are giving up your holdings to increase cash flow. Another example is investing money back into your business. As you make more you can pay your employees more, spend more on marketing, and so on. These activities will boost your cash flow and your business to boot. A third common example is investing in certifications and degrees. This can be done wrong, but if done right will increase your earning power and your cash flow. Make enough moves like this and your cash flow will grow larger and larger over time. It's possible to have an exponential or infinite effect if you pour it all right back in.

If you never invest in cash flow, you will always be working and scrounging. You will either be functionally scraping coins into a savings bucket, living month to month, or both. Using your holdings to boost your cash flow to boost your holdings to boost your cash flow will totally change your life, allowing you to take control of your money and time to focus on health, happiness, and love.

SOCIAL MEDIA FOLLOWERS DO ACTUALLY MATTER

Social media followers do matter- somewhat. They are an audience to make an impact and a measure of your reach. They are a resource that can be tapped if you choose to. It's an optional resource- you don't have to go that route. And many people who collect followers do very little with them. But if you consciously collect followers to make a difference you will be able to monetize and use your audience to boost your income, launch a business, and as a social safety net. Social media followers can be your route to wealth and freedom.

Collecting social media followers is about more than just some number on a screen. It's about real connections. It's a tool for influence. Fake followers for fake connections and fake influence is worthless. A disengaged audience is not particularly useful either. But 1000 true followers can make a tremendous difference- for them and for you. Here is your vessel to make an impact and to be rewarded for it.

The key to collecting followers is to put yourself out there on the internet. And do it in a joyful, loving way. Putting out negative energy won't help you much. It can attract views, but not the kind you want. If you share useful and entertaining stuff, the people who benefit will keep coming back from more. Some of them will talk to their friends about it and things will grow.

Put yourself out there with the intention of being helpful and watch your real connection count grow. You don't have to do anything with it right away, but it's a long-term investment. It can be extremely useful later, depending on what your plan is. Don't just seek numbers on social media. See it as an opportunity to make a difference.

SPEND YOUR MONEY WELL

Making money is pointless if you don't know how to spend it. Money isn't to have, it's to use. There's people out there who make tons of money yet live unhappy lives. Money does correlate with happiness, but that's not a guarantee. You want to maximize it whether you're getting a lot or a little. This all comes down to having a spending strategy that prioritizes making your life better for you and those close around you. You can use your money to improve your time, your health, and the time and health of those who you choose. Or you can waste it on things that are nice but you don't need. Understanding how to spend money is an important key to maximizing your wealth.

The first thing you should plan to spend your money is on better food for better health, energy, and performance. This is the most immediate investment to get an instantly better life, health, and good chance of improving your earning quality. A lot of people underestimate the importance of diet and try to save money on it. You know you want an expensive body, so that's the best investment. Spending more on food doesn't mean necessarily going and eating out at restaurants and throwing a big tip. Buy higher quality food and ingredients. You can eat high quality meat of healthy animals instead of mass produced sick animals. You can eat local organic produce instead of mass produced monocrops, and so on. This is a small habit that will make a huge difference.

The second thing you should plan to spend your money on is a better living situation. You spend some time every single day where you live and there is a massive difference between a good living situation and a bad living situation. You will experience this daily and immediately. This doesn't necessarily mean spending extra money just for a better view. Live with the right people in the right place. It's about improving your everyday environment.

The top priority of immediate spending should be improving your days in the short and long term. Health and living situation are great examples of this.

But there are other things that fall into this category. For example, nice fitting clothes that you will wear on a regular basis or a surfboard that you will use three times a week. Don't underestimate the return on improved living experience.

Another way to improve your life with spending is through generosity to your family and oldest friends. If you have the ability, it will bring you great fulfillment to provide to those who provided for you. It will feel great to fly your friends or family out for a trip. It's worth it to treat them to dinner. This will feel great in the short term but is also a great long-term investment. The same people who you hooked up will have your back in the future when you're down.

You should save some money to have a cash buffer for comfort. If you don't have this, you will create stress. Living paycheck to paycheck isn't fun. But you don't need to hoard it either. Six months savings is plenty. You want to keep it flowing as much as possible. Invest back in your cash flow, keep a nice buffer, and you're good. You may want to make financial investments that could help you later in life, but don't do this at the cost of high quality food and living environment that will immediately improve your life. You want to make your long term better, but you will get cascading benefits from better health.

The main emphasis of wealth is usually on the making money. People forget planning on how to spend it. It makes a difference. You can live a rich life from a little, or a poor life from a lot, depending on how you spend it. So make a plan and make the most of your money!

WATCH YOUR BASKET

Watch your basket or it could disappear. Keep an eye on your bag or it could get stolen. Life might be nice but you could lose it overnight. You could lose your job, you could lose your business, you could lose your cash flow, you could lose your situation and position. Don't get too confident or comfortable. Stay vigilant. Pay attention. Watch your basket for long enough and you increase your chances of your eggs hatching.

If you watch the basket it's fine to put all your eggs in there. It's better than the alternative of throwing eggs in a bunch of different places and hoping if you come back they'll still be there. A farmer literally collects all the separate eggs from the coup and puts them in one basket. It's much easier to carry and watch one basket. The farmer takes care of that basket until it's eaten or out to market.

Monitor your basket. Check your bank balance and project out to the future. Keep an eye on your performance metrics. Check in with your supervisors, employees, teammates, contractors, and associates to see how things are going. Pay attention to the market. Keep your eyes open for everything bad that could happen and you'll be able to see things in advance to protect yourself. There's no magic secret that will punish you for thinking of your eggs getting crushed. Honest thinking is necessary to take precautions.

Watching your basket will allow you to put most or all your eggs safely in that basket. It's what will allow you to move into one career and master it. It will allow you to have one committed relationship. It will let you take care of and protect your body. Backup plans are nice, but too many and you will be distracted from the primary plan. It's fine to be all in if you keep paying attention to be sure that you will make it. Keep an eye on things and you will eventually get there.

START TODAY

Don't procrastinate on your work dreams. Get started today. If you know your dream career, make moves today. If you want to start your business, take some action today. If you must quit your job, maybe you can't do it today, but you can make a timeline plan today. If you don't get started in the present, you won't get started in the future, and you can't get started in the past. The moment is how we experience life, so you have to make moves in the moment. Yesterday was the best day to start, but the second best is today, so get moving or it won't ever happen.

There may be some obstacles that are stopping you from getting started. Maybe you're in a slump. Maybe you have financial burdens. Maybe you feel you're too far down a path. All this may be partially true, but there's still something you can do. Maybe you can't make the full big move today, but you can start thinking about it. You can start studying for that next step. You can make a plan for how you can improve your position to make that leap. Surely you can do something today, and if you do something today every single day, your success will become inevitable.

TURN BAD INTO GOOD

You can turn bad into good. You can turn closing doors into opportunities. You can turn loss into victory. You can turn controversy into massive free marketing. Most people won't do this. Most people take the victim position. Others take the loser position. Maybe there's virtue in being a victim, but it won't take you far. It's much better to play the comeback story.

Obstacles make eventual success more interesting, so make it part of your story. If you ever hit bottom make it a goal to bounce up higher than you've ever bounced before. If you can do this, you will become close to invincible and success will be inevitable.

The first key to turning bad into good is believing that you can and you will. Tell yourself the comeback story. Engrain it in your mind. If you don't do this, you won't look for ways to come back. It won't happen automatically. You have to actively look for it, and it can take a long while. It won't happen overnight. It could be months or even years. But it helps if you are confident that you will eventually get to a point where you can look back on it and see the incident as a turning point for growth.

Take it from me- I've been through multiple public controversies resulting in firings and blacklisting in the niche Magic: the Gathering industry. Each time I turned it into free marketing and a major win. The first time, when I lost my blog job, I used that attention to launch my coaching business. When I got suspended from the Pro Tour I was able to move into full time organic farming and living in Hawaii, which is what I wanted to do. The incidents were painful at the time but that's the way growth is. I could have wallowed on it, but I turned the tables and came out the victor. This is possible for you.

The actual strategy for turning bad into good will be nuanced and vary heavily depending on the circumstance, but the basic story will be the same. A lost job turns into entrepreneurship. A suspension results in preferred life change. A lost relationship leads to a better relationship. And so on. This is all possible, and the key is to believe that it will happen. You will open the door in your mind to turn bad into good, and every situation will turn out great.

HAPPINESS

BE HAPPY WITH WHAT YOU HAVE

Be happy with what you have. Give thanks for the things you have. Be happy to even be alive. Ideally you have your health, wealth, and love secured and it will be easy to be happy. But even if you don't have these things it's not too late to get started on being happy right now. And when you have those things don't forget how lucky you are. Be happy with what you have, because you have a whole lot when you could have nothing.

Make a list of all the things you have. It's a lot. Many people forget. They take it for granted. We all do it. We get stressed out over small things. It's normal because we have to attend to the details of life. But every day it's good to take a step back and drink it all in. You are alive. You can read this. You have clothes. You have made it this far. You have a lot going for you. There's reason to celebrate and be happy right now.

Happiness comes more easily when you have the things that contribute to happiness. But it's okay when you don't. Go for happiness every single day. Make plays for it. Don't wait on it. Don't push off happiness. Every bad day can be salvaged. You can find a moment at the end of every day to be happy with what you have.

UNLOCKING HAPPINESS

Happiness comes easily with health and good work and creates the condition for love. Health is our vehicle and controls much of our moods. While money does contribute to happiness, fulfilling work that contributes meaningfully to society is just as important. Once we have control of our health and work life happiness comes naturally.

Love can contribute to happiness. But love is not a good fix for unhappiness. In many cases love can cause or multiply unhappiness. Love arises more easily when certain conditions are right. An empty cup doesn't have much to pour into anyone else's. A full cup of good health and wealth can be poured into another's cup. Focus first on filling your own cup to make yourself happy. Later with a full cup you will have much more to love with to make others happy.

DO THINGS THAT MAKE YOU HAPPY

Do things that make you happy. Do things that bring you joy. Do things that put you in a better mood. Do them every single day. Make it a ritual. No matter how the day is going you have can make it a good one by doing things that boost your mood. Have some go-tos- a workout, a place you can go, an activity, a group.

Figure out what you like and program it into your days. Go out of your way to do things that make you happy and you will experience more happiness.

This may seem obvious but not everyone is doing it. People get distracted by small things and let the day slip from them. Or we do things that distract us rather than make us happy. Instead of going for a run with the dog you could sit on social media. It's your choice. Or people don't know what makes them happy. If that's you then you haven't tried enough things. might not find out that you like a certain hobby, career, or activity until you try it. There's so many to try that you have to start experimenting. It may take years to find your thing, but once you know then you can bring yourself joy daily.

There are certain things you should do every day, and activities that make you happy belong on that list. The days are better when we give thanks, take care of our bodies and minds, do fulfilling work and are rewarded, love and are loved, and do things that make us happy. So go get after it today!

HAPPINESS IS A WAY OF THINKING

Happiness is heavily influenced by certain conditions. But why do some seem to be happy with poor health and wealth? Why are some people who have it all still unhappy? There's more to it . Happiness is a way of thinking. Happiness is a way of looking at the world. Happiness is a way of interfacing with society. Happiness is a way of being.

Thinking happy starts with thinking happy thoughts. Think about what you're grateful for. Think about what you have. Think about how far you've made it. Think about all the people who have helped you along the way. Think optimistically of the possibilities of the future. Do these things regularly and you will be much happier. Many people do these things, many people do not. You can do this and it will contribute to your happiness.

Use specific mental strategies to think happy, such as reframing, deflecting, and combating negative thoughts. Most people have the occasional internal dialogue of negative self-talk. You may hear from an internal voice how you are not good enough, are a loser, ought to quit, and so on. You may not be able to ever fully eliminate these thoughts, but you can make the most of them. You can complete them to make them more optimistic. You can counter them, arguing back if necessary. You can ask them to go away and come back with something more useful. You can state the positive opposite five times as much. The internal battle may never stop, but you can still win it, to be happy one day at a time.

HAPPINESS COMES AND GOES

Happiness comes and goes. You can't be happy all the time. You will have to feel all the other emotions. Some of them positive, many of them negative. You will feel pain, fear, anger, and despair from time to time. But you will feel happy again. Emotions are waves. They don't last forever. Your goal is to experience more happiness more consistently. To experience some happiness daily. Not to be happy all the time, because that's not possible. When you feel bad, it's okay, because that's part of it. The valleys accentuate the peaks.

If you were happy all the time you wouldn't get nearly as much done. Too much contentment causes stagnation. If you're eternally happy, what will drive you to work hard? What will encourage you to improve your situation? The negative emotions have an important function. They tell you that not all is right and you can do better. The spur you into action. From unhappiness you will do the things necessary to be happy for a time. This is the cycle.

Happiness is temporary, so appreciate it as it comes. When it's gone, have faith that it will come back. Be thankful to experience the full range of emotions because that makes life that much richer. We want a challenge, not an easy ride. We're after success and we must fail on the way too it. We must come from the negative to truly experience happiness. Aim for some happiness every day, but not every moment. It's okay.

THANK THE MORNINGS

Thank the mornings. Give thanks for waking up, because you easily couldn't have. You're very lucky just to wake up in the morning to another day. These days are limited. Give thanks for your body. You have enough health to move today, but not forever. Give thanks for your situation, your family, the kind people in your life, the things you have. Give thanks for the challenges that will make you into a stronger person. Starting the day with gratitude will change your entire frame for the day. The simple practice of thanking the mornings will make you a much happier person.

The best time to give thanks is upon waking, and the best thing to do upon waking is to give thanks. Many successfully happy people recognize this as a keystone habit. Morning thanks sets the tone for the day. You may find yourself giving thanks throughout the day. Other people will feel your gratitude and be happier for it.

Not everyone is thankful. Many people take what they have for granted. They complain about waking up to another imperfect day. They complain about their body and their relationships. They groan upon waking. Imagine how their tune will change on their deathbed. How happy they would be to have all the things they previously took for granted or even complained about. These same people walk around each day without thanking the people around them. They don't receive as much thanks or gratitude either. No thanks, they aren't too happy.

If there's one small habit you could change that would have the biggest impact on your happiness it is this- thanking the mornings. Doing this consistently every day will change your life in a massive way, starting with your mood. If there's a key to happiness, perhaps morning thanks is it.

THANK THE FOOD

Thank the food. Thank the universe for preparing it for you. Thank the earth for growing it. Thank the water and the farmers. Thank the animal. Thank the plant. Thank the cook and the server. Think about what you can do with this food. Think about if you didn't have any food. This simple routine before each meal adds a lot to happiness. When you are grateful for every meal, it's hard to be too mad about things. Thanking the food puts it in perspective.

Too many people take their food for granted. They eat it without thanking it. They don't consider everything that had to happen to bring the food to them. They complain over their meals and stress out about the bills. Unhappiness is too common, especially among people who don't thank the food.

Get yourself a routine for thanking the food. Do it in the mornings. Do it before each meal. Take a moment of silence, song, or prayer. Speak it out loud or think it to yourself. Thank the food and the community around it. Eat it, enjoy it, and be happy!

THANK THE PEOPLE

Thank the people. Let them know you appreciate them. Let them know you care. Let them know you see them. Thank them for everything they do for you. The small things. People don't get thanked that often so they will appreciate you for this. It's a small act but it can have a big effect. Not only will it make their day better, but it will have a butterfly effect. They will start to show more appreciation and give more thanks. It can change the whole culture of your social circles and organizations. You can make a huge impact with this one small thing. When you thank people, they will be thankful for it.

Most people take other people for granted. Most people don't even see the other people around them. They're in their own little worlds. They don't notice the small things. So they don't give thanks. This is the standard in society. It's also why small acts go such a long way- they're unusual. It's too bad how society can be, but it makes it very easy for an individual to stand out. All you must do is the small acts of thanks and people will feel seen and appreciated.

Thank people for the hard work they've been doing. Thank them for passing the salt. Thank them for being on time. Thank them for thinking of you. Thank them for sending you a picture. Thank them for being them. Do it consistently and watch the thanks and appreciation flow back your way. It will raise up everyone's happiness, especially your own!

THANK YOURSELF

Thank yourself. Give yourself a pat on the back. Give yourself a hug. Give yourself some love and affection. Give yourself some words of encouragement- you've made it this far! Thank yourself for all the struggles you've gone through to make it here today. You did it!

No one will care about your wellbeing as much as you. Maybe your parents will love you a lot, but it's still you living in your body and it's up to you to make the most of it. No one is going to force you to do the things you need to do to be happier. No one is going to appreciate what you've done to get here as much as you. No one knows you like you know you. You must care for yourself. You are the most important person in your corner. You are the most reliable person in your life. You show up every day and you owe yourself thanks for it.

It's too easy to engage in self-loathing. Many people do this. They talk shit to themselves. They put themselves down. They blame themselves. While some of this discord is natural to drive us to success, it can also tear us down from the inside and set us up for failure. You must have good self-talk. At times you need to be real with yourself. The rest of the time give yourself some thanks. Be grateful that you're here with you. Thank yourself.

TAKE RESPONSIBILITY FOR YOUR SITUATION

Take responsibility for your situation. You are in control of your reality. Don't blame other people or bad luck. You're getting what you're putting out. It's all on you. Yes you did have some luck from above to even be here, and your parents and early experiences had a massive effect on you. But you aren't a child anymore. You're a man and that means taking responsibility. The moment you choose to be in control of your situation, you start to see what you can do to better serve others, rather than wonder why certain things happen to you. Taking responsibility leads to massive growth.

Many people do not take responsibility. They blame the weather. They blame the government. They blame the traffic. They blame bad luck. They curse God. They focus on everything outside of their control instead of spending time to look what they could have done better. External gratitude is a good thing, but external blame is a way to get stuck in the mud by yourself. Forget all the outside forces. They don't control you. You control you.

Taking responsibility requires looking deeper at your actions. If you got a bad result maybe you didn't put in a good effort. If you got a negative reaction maybe you had a bad approach. If you keep getting fired, maybe you're a bad employee. The list goes on and on. There's no problem admitting mistakes. That's how we grow. When things don't go well, assume there's something you could have done better and you will always find one.

Taking full responsibility for your situation may not be entirely truthful, but it's entirely useful.

The truth is that the wind will blow us about. But it's not a helpful way of thinking. Believing that you are the leaf and the wind may not be totally true, but it is a great way of thinking. You will always be looking for self-improvement. Taking responsibility is a massive key to growth on the road to happiness.

ASK FOR DIRECTIONS IN LIFE

Ask for directions in life. Don't wander around lost. You don't have to figure everything out yourself. You'll figure it out a lot faster if you have mentors to look up to. Ask people questions. Especially those people who have what you want. Ask them how they did it. Their success is a possible blueprint for you to follow. You don't have to copy all the advice you get. Some of it may not be for you. But a lot of it will be. Asking for directions will get you to your destination faster.

Some people drive around aimlessly looking for their destination because they're too cool to ask for directions. These same people drift around on the seas of life without going anywhere in particular. It's not enough to have the vehicle. You must know where you're going. A smart pilot looks up the map and considers the possible routes. At that point you can choose your path. It's much easier once you know your options. Check the map.

You don't have to try everything yourself to find out if it works. There's way too many possible mistakes you can make. Too many dead ends. You want to learn from your mistakes, but it's even better to learn from other people's mistakes. Study the wrong turns that people made in life. Look at where their path veered off. For many people, the problem is not asking for directions.

The most successful people asked for directions. They had mentors. They had teachers. They had teammates. They took counsel. Even the pioneers who went in new directions projected what might happen. People who wandered off cliffs didn't come back. People who took native guides came back with their lives and maps of the land. Never take life alone. Seek help. Ask for directions. You'll get there much sooner.

FIRST BREAK YOUR FEARS THEN FOLLOW YOUR GUT

First break your fears, then follow your gut. The transition from boyhood to manhood requires courage. Courage requires fear. You will have to step out of your comfort zone and do things that make you feel very uncomfortable. These things might include approaches, phone calls, offers, going to events, traveling, and more. If you avoid these things, you will stay a boy, so you must get used to acting in the face of discomfort. However, maturing as a man requires recognizing your strengths and weaknesses, assessing the situation, and avoiding doing weird and uncomfortable shit. Over time, some things that were previously scary will become normal daily behaviors. Other actions that felt very uncomfortable will still feel very uncomfortable. Listen to your gut on these things and don't act. Your gut feeling is a protection from real physical danger, financial danger, social danger, and emotional danger. For a time you must go against your gut, but as you learn yourself, you must follow your gut.

Growing from boyhood to manhood does involve doing uncomfortable shit. As kids we have built in fears to protect us- fear of strangers, fear of unknown foods, fear of getting hurt. These fears help us reach adolescence alive but no longer serve us after that. We need to man up and act despite this fear. We must take scary actions. Sometimes you must act even if your heart is pounding, your hands are sweating, and your stomach hurts. Over time as you survive these events the fear disappears. Your brain realizes that it's okay. These actions become normal. You will lose your fear of public speaking. You will lose your fear of interviews and phone calls. You will lose your fear of the dentist. You will lose your fear of showing up to events alone. But some fears you will not lose.

The more experience you have as a man, the more you must go back to trusting your gut. For certain things your gut instinct will never change, and you should begin to trust that it is right. The boyhood to manhood transition is aided by brute force, but maturation requires more discernment. You will have to change your behaviors and stop acting despite discomfort. The same habits that helped you become a man will no longer serve you. If you feel uncomfortable about selling everything you own and putting it all into an unproven business, you should listen to that discomfort. If you feel uncomfortable about scaling a rock face with no harness, it's for a very good reason. If you get a bad vibe from a relationship you should trust to walk away.

You do want to hit home runs in life, but the best way to do that is to get more at bats. You don't want to strike out and you don't want the game to end. Your gut instinct will save you from the strike outs and the game losing plays. Once you have some experience, you'll know. Trust your feelings- they may not have been right as a boy, but they are right as a man. You'll be happier for it.

SPRING FOLLOWS WINTER

Spring follows winter. Every single time. Times are the coldest, darkest, dampest, slowest, right before they change direction and start getting easier. It happens every year. Never think the bad times will last forever. Always look ahead to the spring. Know that this is temporary and you will get through it if you just keep going. Life is full of seasonal cycles. Things will get bad again, but it won't last forever. Look ahead to spring.

Summer follows spring. So use the spring time to expand and to plant seeds so you have something to harvest in the summer. Summertime is usually easy. But just like every other season, it's temporary. It won't last forever. Don't take it for granted. This too, shall pass. Enjoy it and make the most of it.

Fall follows summer. Things begin to slow down again. The nights get longer. The days get shorter and colder. The last of the harvest wraps up. Winter is coming, so stockpile to prepare. Defend yourself. Make sure you are defended against the elements. Be prepared.

Winter follows fall. Sure, things are dark, but they are temporary. Take this as a time to snuggle up and read. Take a season to contract. Spend the time consuming. Spend the time reading, learning, sleeping, and making plans for the spring. Don't think the dark times will last forever. For spring will follow winter. Every single time.

WATER YOUR LAWN

Water your lawn. Tend to your garden. Make your own grass greener. Don't worry too much about the grass on the other side. Focus on upgrading your current situation step by step. Very occasionally the grass is greener on the other side and it will pay off to make a big move. But most of the time the constant vigilance and searching to trade up is a loss- it eats energy and causes you to neglect your current situation. Better to make what you have better. You will be happier for it.

Is the grass greener somewhere out there? Maybe. To find it you will have to put in a lot of time and energy. And you might not find it. It's sometimes worth it to look. More often you'll make your current situation worse looking for something that you won't find. You have what you need around you. Maybe not everything you want, but you can make this work. And you can certainly make it better by putting in the effort.

Put in consistent work to improve your life. Water the lawn of your body. Water the lawn of your work. Water the lawn of your business. Water the lawn of your relationships. Keep pouring in vital nutrients to make the plants grow. Eventually they will produce fruit. It can take many years, decades even. But if you keep switching around you'll never be able to log the years to make it worth it.

There may be something better for you out there. But you can make what you currently have better than that. Focus on what's in front of you. Put in the time to make it better.

AIM FOR GOOD TODAYS

Aim for good todays. Make it a goal for today to be the best day it can. Do what you can to start it off right and end it on a good note. Going for good days will make a good life. String off enough good days and you have good years. Life is for living, not for pushing off until you're old. You should be having good days today and for as long as possible. If every day is a good day, you will be happy.

What makes a day good? It means different things to different people but there are some fundamentals. A good day presents a physical challenge. A good day presents a mental challenge. A good day has success. A good day works and plays with fun people you like. A good day involves learning new things. A good day can involve mastering old things. A good day could involve intimate time with a loved partner. A good day probably involves some time outside in nature. Good days come in all shapes and sizes. Not all good days will look the same. They may be totally different. But they share some of these basic things in common.

Prioritize work that is enriching to your life. If you love your work you will have many good days. If you hate your work, you will be miserable. Good work prioritizes health and fun as well. It should be good for you so you feel good for a longer time. It should allow for fun loving relationships with your workmates. If you love what you work for, what you're doing, and who you're doing it with, you 'll be happy.

Too many people make the mistake of aiming for good tomorrows. They sacrifice today every day and suddenly they string a bunch of bad days into a bad life. Some sacrifice is okay but too much sacrifice of the present is not worth it. This is your life and it should be fun to live. Don't sacrifice tomorrow too much either because then your good days will run out. Project into the future. Some balance is necessary. Go for good todays that build towards good tomorrows. Don't be all invested in the future but invest somewhat. You're likely to live longer and you want many good happy days for a long happy life.

GET TO THE RIGHT LOCATION

Get to the right location. As soon as possible. The right location is the place that you will bloom the best. Cactus grows best in the desert. Mango grows best in the tropics. There is a best place for you. For many people this is the place you were born. For many of us it's not. Our seed was scattered randomly, and while we develop deep roots with the place we grew up, it's not always the right place for us. This matters a lot. The wrong place does not give the best career options. The wrong place will not lead to the best love relationships because the right person won't be there. You have to get to the place that is best for you to flourish. It may require research and travel, but it is worth it.

Just because you were born somewhere does not mean it is the best place for you to live as an adult. You were there because of random circumstances. Staying rooted there could be a huge mistake. You may not have the best circumstances there to achieve your full potential. For example, if you are very pale you will burn around the equator and be forced to stay inside, but if you are very dark you will do well, and vice versa. This is just one factor. Don't think you need to stay where you grew up. Gather the information of where you might better grow and gather the resources to make it happen.

As opportunity presents itself, travel. Travel to places you think you might live. When you are there, explore the idea of living there. You can start off with a short trip. You don't have to do it all at once. If it feels right, make a plan to move out there. If it's not right, keep looking. It will take time and resources but it's worth it. It's a key to your work and your happiness. Once you find the place you can develop longer term loving relationships. If you develop these relationships before finding the right place, you may have to terminate them when you move. Follow the proper sequence. Search for and find the right place first. This place will make you happier. Once you're there, the rest will fall into place.

GOOD ENOUGH IS PERFECT

Good enough is perfect. It doesn't have to be perfect. It just has to be good enough. Perfect is too elusive. It's not real. There will always be problems. There will always be some issues. Don't let those problems and issues detract you from what you do have. Life is about tradeoffs, compromise, and sacrifice. You can't have it all. You shouldn't have to. Don't go for perfect. Go for good enough!

Most of the time perfect is not actually possible. In the rare times when it is, the extra time investment to get from 95% to 100% isn't worth it. You get diminishing returns for that. Those extra hours could have been spent improving other areas of your life from not good enough to good enough. That extra couple % at the top is not necessary and is often impossible.

You should be striving for good enough in every pillar of your life. You want your health to be good enough. There will always be some issues, some injuries, some problems. Try to stay as healthy as you can. You're looking for good enough in your work. It will never be perfect. There will always be something lacking in compensations, work relationships, work lifestyle, and so on. Perfect work isn't possible, but good work is. You're looking for good enough happiness. You can't be happy all the time. You will experience the full range of emotions. But if you can have some happiness and fulfillment every day, that will be good enough. You are looking for good enough in your romantic relationships. There's no perfect match. There will be problem behaviors and areas of friction. There may be hard times of the month. That's okay. Those problems won't ruin all the other good that you have unless you try to be perfect. Instead focus on the good. You'll see that you can have good enough. And good enough is perfect!

YOU DON'T HAVE TO BE PERFECT

You don't have to be perfect. You can't be perfect. Good enough is just fine. You are guaranteed to make mistakes. Don't dwell on them too much. Try to learn from them and move on. View your imperfections and mistakes as areas for learning. Focus more on your strengths. Trying to be perfect is a good way to waste energy as you fail, because it's just not possible. You have flaws. Everyone has flaws. It's okay. You don't have to be perfect. You're good enough.

Do the best that you can today. If you screw up, come back and try again tomorrow. Don't worry about past mistakes. Focus on future opportunities. Don't compare yourself to other people. Look at how much you've grown. Don't strive to be perfect. Strive to do better. Don't make it a goal to never make a mistake. Make it a goal to learn from every mistake. Don't try to be perfect. Just do your best and keep on going. You're good enough.

SOME SACRIFICE IS OKAY

Some sacrifice is okay. Life is about tradeoffs and compromise. You'll have to give up some stuff that you want to get what you need. There's no way around it. You can't have your cake and eat it. A life without sacrifice won't lead anywhere great. But too much sacrifice can be bad. Give up your good present for the promise of a better future and it may never come. That's not a good tradeoff. Sacrificing some of your time and energy is okay, but not all of it.

Sacrifice is necessary to progress in many areas of life. You can't reach your healthiest potential without giving up sweet and tasty garbage food. You can't do it without giving up time so that you can work out. You can't launch a business without sacrificing some weekends. You can't master your craft without giving up a lot of other opportunities. There are opportunity costs to everything, and to succeed you will have to evaluate the costs and give up everything but the essentials.

Be careful not to sacrifice too much for questionable returns. Try not to sacrifice your health. It's not worth it for almost anything. Try not to sacrifice your whole present days- this is a bad habit to get into because it can make for a bad life. Compromise is a balance. You have to give up some to get some. But don't give up everything. Don't sacrifice it all. Some sacrifice is plenty.

SURF THE WAVES OF THE MIND

Surf the waves of the mind. You can't stop the waves. You can't fight the current. You gotta flow with the waves of the mind. The same thoughts come and go. You can't stop the thoughts, but you can identify them and go with them. They won't last forever. You can watch them pass. Fighting repetitive thoughts consumes a lot of energy. But if you let it happen things will be a lot easier.

The mind works in mysterious ways. Why do the same thoughts pop up over and over again? Why do we hear the same phrases? Why do we picture the same faces? Why do we ruminate and stress? These are good questions. But "how do we stop these thoughts" is not a good question. They are a part of life. You can't stop them. You can give them as much energy as you like. You can struggle upstream fighting them, or just let the energy pass.

The key to surfing the waves of the mind is to be okay with the waves. It can be hard to even accept that the waves will keep coming. We hope they go away forever. We focus on the waves. When we accept the mind's waves things become much easier. We can focus on our own actions that we take with the thoughts. In this way it's possible to be happy even with bothersome thoughts. They're just passing and they don't define you. What you do with the thoughts defines you.

TURN MISFORTUNE INTO A SUCCESS STORY

Turn misfortune into a success story. Things are going to go wrong. Sometimes it's your fault, sometimes it's bad luck, often it's a mixture of the two. You will be set back. Maybe you get injured, get fired, or get dumped. There's opportunities to learn here. You could be a sad victim or you could figure out what you could have done better and move forward. You could let the story end there or you can keep going until you're better off than before. You can turn your worst moments into catalyst to blast off to your best. People love a good rag to riches story too. The lower the valley the higher the peak will be. So when things go wrong it's okay, you'll bounce back stronger than before.

Frame your story so that you are the hero of your life. Don't be the victim of your life. Don't be a bystander. Don't be a leaf in the wind. Take as much control as you can. If you get pooped on, maybe it's because you were in the wrong place. You can do better. You can position yourself better. You can take better actions. You can get to a point where you tell your story with a laugh. You'll be able to say "look how far I came" and know it was for the best.

Major failure isn't necessary, but it is usually inevitable. Some people do a better job of dodging it. But if you are going to swing for the fences you will risk striking out. You may need to fail your way to success. It's not for everyone, but those with the thick skin to keep powering on through will get the chips in the end. Any bad beats that happen to you are not the end of the story- they are the end of a chapter setting up for an epic comeback story. It's never too late for a comeback and that's how you should think about setbacks in life. Even if you lose everything and are shamed across the internet you can come back from it. Take your lumps and just keep on going. You'll make a better story this way.

SWING FOR THE FENCES!

Swing for the fences! Go for the home run. All you need is one so keep on swinging. Life is short and you only have one opportunity at this. Play for the maximum possible upside. Makes moves for the best possible situation. Think about what a home run means to you and go for it. Go for your ideal life. Go for your ideal body. Go for your ideal career. Go for your ideal relationship. It won't happen overnight and it might not happen at all. But if you swing for the fences there's a chance you actually hit a home run. If you don't swing for the fences you can't get there at all. If you strike out it's okay because there's more chances. Keep swinging!

Don't play too defensively in life. Don't play too small ball either. Incremental improvements are fine, but they should be small changes towards your best possible deal. Don't settle for bad. Don't settle for mediocre. This sort of strategy leads to a medium life. Medium is okay if you didn't only have one shot. At least if you try for the best you have a chance, and if you come up short you'll probably go farther than you would have otherwise. Play for the win. Swing for home runs.

PICK GOOD PEOPLE FOR YOUR CIRCLE

Pick good people for your circle. Pick people who will build you up. Pick people who have your back. Pick people who will help you up when you need it. Pick people who will inspire you to grow and motivate you to achieve. Who we spend our time with has an enormous influence on who we become. If we pick the wrong people we could be dragged down. So be careful when choosing who to let into your life and how deep to go with them. If you pick the right people you will become much more successful, learn faster, and be happier.

Not everyone discriminates when it comes to the circle. They let in anyone who is around. They let in people with bad habits who infect them with the same. They let in people with bad attitudes which bleed over to them. They let in people who demotivate them and create obstacles for their goals. The whole group becomes stagnant. It's sad, but it doesn't have to be this way. If you actively pick your circle you will be on the fast track.

You don't have to kick everyone out and cut people out of your life to do this. Family is family and coworkers are coworkers. You don't have full control over who is around. You have some control and you should work with that. And importantly you control how deep you go. You control how much extra time and energy you spend. It's your choice what to do with your free time. It's your choice who to hang out with off work. It's your choice who to call when you want advice.

A good circle will grow itself. The right people bring in more of the right people. You introduce them to each other, they introduce you to them. The circle grows. A cancerous circle does the same thing, so be careful. It will either get better and better or worse and worse. So pick the people who make your life better.

Spend more time with them. Meet their friends. You will be happier for it.

PLEASE A FEW

Please a few. Don't try to please everyone. You can't do it. Try to help the people who you care most about. Try to help the people who care most about you. Try to help the people who will return the favor. Try to help the people who want to be helped. Try to please the people who are easy to please. This is a mission you can succeed in.

You can't make everyone happy. People have other stuff going on besides you. It's not all about you. You can't make everyone like you. Some people won't like you. It's not a big deal. It's just the way it is. Don't get caught up in it. Don't spend a bunch of energy on the people who just don't care. It's a waste of time. You only have so much to give so don't think about it. Spend your precious time and energy on the people who will appreciate what you're doing. Choose who you want to please and help them out. You can't make everyone happy, but you can make a few happy.

GROW THICK SKIN

Grow thick skin. You are going to need it to be protected from the harsh words of the world. If you are too sensitive your emotions will be like a leaf in the wind. Grow thick skin so you can be a rock on the ground, immune to any weather. This will allow you to be less reliant on external factors for happiness. Growing thick skin will help you take control of your world.

Human sociability comes with empathy, meaning emotional contagion. We tend to feel what those around us feel. When people are mean to us, we get mad. Angry people trigger something in us. Thrown tomatoes make us see red. This is normal for most people. But it is possible to take mastery of the situation. You can counter with calm. You can catch the tomato. You diffuse the situation.

Empathy will help you feel where the other person is coming from. Conscious empathy will allow you to feel from a distance. Someone being mad doesn't mean you have to be mad. You have a choice. You can take a step back and think about their situation. They most likely have some problems going on in their life-perhaps a health problem that negatively affects their mood. Maybe a work problem that is making them struggle. Their problem aren't your problems. Their emotions aren't your emotions. Their words aren't your words.

The more barbs you take, the more calluses you will develop, the thicker your skin, the more you will be protected from mean words. It is a painful process, but it gets less painful. In time you will be able to see the other's problems and serve them. But first you must grow thick skin to protect yourself. Grow thick skin and your happiness will be protected.

BE HAPPY LOSING

Be happy losing. Get used to it. Losing is a big part of life. You will lose a lot. You will have health setbacks. You will have wealth setbacks. You will lose love and you will lose some happiness. It's part of the voyage. It's supposed to be challenging. It's not gonna be easy very often. These losses will sting, but you can't get too down on them. Be happy to learn from them. Be happy that you took action instead of doing nothing. Be happy that you loved. Be happy that you have another chance to get up and do it again.

If you get too upset losing you will have a rough life. You will either become extremely frustrated over the various losses, or you will stop acting out of fear of losing. It is better to win, but it's just not possible to win all the time. We often don't learn enough from our victories either because they don't force introspection. It's a balance. You must be okay with losing so that you keep taking shots. Don't give up no matter how much you lose, just be happy that you have another shot and keep going.

FIND YOUR TRIBE

Find your tribe. Find the people who make sense to you. Surround yourself with the people you click with. Humans are tribal. You're not meant to be isolated. Social circle determines much of our happiness. It helps to have the right people around you. People you connect to with similar interests. A community. From your tribe you can pick your circle and deeper relationships. The tribe is already screened for people who are relatable to you so the percentage of deeper relationships is way higher. Finding your tribe is one of the biggest social keys.

Your tribe doesn't have to look like you. It's more important that they think like you. They're into the same sorts of things. They see the world through similar lenses. You do want to expose yourself to other points of view. You don't want to go too inbred into echo chambers. But if you don't see eye to eye there's only so close you can get.

You can find your tribe through interest groups- volunteer days, weekly meetups, events. Know what sort of activity you want to do and go there. You know the people who will be there are interested in the same thing. You can meet them and continue to see them. Ask around. Use the internet to locate events. Show up, even if you must do it alone. You won't stay alone for long if you go. The surest way to stay alone is to keep to yourself. So go out and meet your tribe!

MODERATION > ABSTINENCE > EXCESS

Moderations beats abstinence beats excess. Too much of anything will hurt you. Way too much of anything will kill you. On the other hand, abstinence tends towards isolation. Isolation will kill you. Moderation is an important life skill. The more moderate people live happier and longer lives. Some people don't think it's possible because they didn't learn self-control themselves. You can learn and it will make a huge difference for your happiness.

Excess is a huge problem. Drink too much alcohol and it can ruin your life. Play too many video games and you get the same. It goes on for anything. It doesn't mean alcohol and video games are the problem though. If you can stop at one drink and one game there's no problem. They can even improve your lives, giving you a different social outlet. The key is quitting when you say you will quit. You must be consistent with yourself. You have to be true to yourself when you say "one more". You must follow through when you say you are going to take a break to reset your habits. The problem isn't the thing- it's in your habits. It's hard to control, but it's under your control.

The answer for some people is abstinence. They don't drink at all. They don't play any games. They avoid people who do the things they are excessive about. This can be very isolating. Isolation also kills. Social circles are important and you don't want to have to avoid them. You should be able to handle yourself to keep wide social nets.

The key is in moderation. It's all about self-control. It's all about perspective. You must believe you can control yourself. You do have the power. It is up to you. If you are out of control, it's indicative of other problems. It shows that your words aren't good to yourself and they won't be good to other people too. If you can't handle it, you need to work on yourself.

When it comes down to it, abstinence does beat excess. Excess will kill you way faster. Abstinence can be lonely, but it can save your life. Ideally you learn moderation, but if you truly can't, abstinence is reasonable. For many people moderation is learnable though. It comes down to small actions. It's about follow through on your part. Setting obstacles in your path to overdoing it. Setting alarms. Having accountable people in your circle. Having consistent people with good habits around you. Surround yourself with the wrong people with the wrong habits and excess is sure to follow. You may have to exit some circles, but not all of them. Create some space. Surround yourself with moderate people. Study their habits. See what they do and copy them. It is possible to learn moderation. And if you do learn moderation you will be happier for it.

TODAY MAY BE YOUR LAST DAY (BUT PROBABLY ISN'T)

Today might be your last day, although it probably won't be. You're likely to live longer. But you may get hit by lightning, a truck, a ballistic missile, or just drop dead. You don't know. Eventually one day will be your last day, and it could be today. You can't treat every day like it's your last day. You can't tie up every loose end every single day. But you can make an effort to end the day on a good note. You should be grateful for the day, just to be alive, because you're lucky to have it. Make the most of it. Put in the extra effort. Say "I love you". But don't assume you won't have to wake up tomorrow and go back to work, so don't burn your bridges today either. Make the most of today but keep plans to be alive tomorrow too.

Sometimes people see the end coming far in advance, often it ends abruptly. That's been the way of life and death. We are all going to pass, some sooner than others. Many people never got the privilege to be born at all. We're lucky to have that. It's easy to forget how lucky we are just to be here. Sure, there's shit going on that will cause some anxiety and suck some energy. But don't let it ruin the experience of being alive. It's wonderful, it's temporary, it can end randomly and unexpectedly, so treat it as such. Try not to have too many loose ends that you would regret going out on. Keep things tidy so if the worst happens at least you'll feel good about the life you lived.

At the same time, you will probably be alive tomorrow. You're likely to live some good years too. You ought to plan it out and make some investments in the future. It's worth it to put in some extra energy now to free up extra time later. It's a balance. It's a calculated decision. Don't ruin your future today "because YOLO". Make a good day but take some precautions for the future. You're likely to live for it to pay off. Try to be happy now while putting in some energy to make it easier to be happy later.

BE HAPPILY SINGLE

Be happily single. Enjoy your time alone. Do fun things. Do productive things. Do creative things. Love yourself. Be free. Pursue what you want to pursue. Work on yourself. Do things that make you happy. Build a good life for yourself. Once you are happily single you can start to think about being happily in a relationship. You're ready. But you may not even want it, because the relationship is competing with your happy alone time. It raises the bar for your relationships. It will have to be good to be worth it.

It's too common a mistake to rush into love. To think it will solve your problems. It can actually make them worse. If you are unhappy alone, you will be unhappy together. If you are unhealthy alone, you will be unhealthy together. If you are poor alone, you will be poor together. First you should be healthy, wealthy, and happy by yourself. Once you're here you'll be ready to love others. If you have to wait, that's okay, wait. Work on yourself. Work on your own life. Build something great that you can show to others and bring them into. When you are happy single you will be able to share your happiness with another person.

KEEP GOING, WE'RE GONNA MAKE IT

Keep going, we're gonna make it! Don't give up fam. Thank you universe for the opportunity. We got this. Through good times and bad, keep going. Believe that you will make it in the end. Persist. Keep trying. Get up one more time and go for it again. It's not over til it's over. It's still early in the game and you maximize your chance by just keeping going. Keep moving your feet, you're well on your way.

Happiness is a mindset. From mindset comes actions. From actions come mindset. Despair is to give up. It's sad to quit on something you care about. It's exhausting to not have the energy to make it happen. If you believe, you can achieve. If you keep going you will begin to believe it's possible. If you believe it's possible you will begin to keep going. Let happiness feed your actions; let your actions feed your happiness.

Happiness can mean a lot of things, especially the things that you do. Your mood and your behavior go together. Daily happiness is in the process. You can't wait for long term goals or happiness will be a rare day. Happiness needs to come from the little things that you can control. Not everyone can feed you happiness, but you can produce it yourself by loving yourself to just keep going. You're gonna make it fam!

LOVE

LOVE YOURSELF FIRST

Love yourself first. If you don't love yourself, you won't have any love leftover to share. If you don't love yourself you will be coming to relationships from a place of need rather than generosity. Take care of yourself- your body and mind, your service and reward, your happiness. Once these things are solid you will be in a strong position to love others.

Relationships tend to be multiplicative. Multiply two whole numbers and you have synergistic growth- 2 times 2 equals 4. Multiply fractions and you have negative loss- ½ times ½ equals 1/4th. Too many people are coming from fractional existence to love and are worse off for it. In these situations each partner can grow worse from the relationship. They share bad habits and negative ways of thinking. It's better to take a step back and work on yourself. You shouldn't be coming to a relationship to make you whole or you will make each other less. It's okay to be alone for a while as you level up. As you perform more consistent acts of love for yourself you will slowly find yourself in a position to truly love others.

Good loving relationships will contribute to our happiness. But love is not a great answer to unhappiness. Each party can become more and more unhappy in such a relationship. The love rich get richer, the love poor get poorer. The road up is through self-love. Love yourself more and you will have more love to give.

Make sure you are doing everything for yourself first. If you are in poor physical health, how can you help feed others? If you don't have enough money for yourself, who will you support others? If you aren't happy, how will you help others in their happiness? If you don't love yourself, how can you love others? It's simple. Take care of yourself. Love yourself first. Love others next.

LOVE MANY

Love many. Spread out your love. Diversify your love. Love yourself. Pour your love into friends and family. Love her, but not her only. Don't become reliant on one person for love. Don't put all your eggs in someone else's basket who can walk away with it. Put your love in several baskets. This way you aren't reliant on one person for your social needs. You won't tend towards toxic codependency or wrecked by bad breakups. If your social net fills your needs you will have consistent love.

Intimate relationships should be allowed to go deep. But they shouldn't crowd out friendships and family. They should be loving, but not the sole source of love. They should be affectionate, but you should have affection outside too. They may be sexual, but you should at least be able to take care of that yourself also when you need to. Your love relationships should be enriching, but they can't fill every lack. Spread out your love.

Make a conscious effort to spread out your love. Call up friends and family you haven't interacted with recently. Try for more loving touch and affection in friendly relationships. Aim to understand and be understood by a wider circle. Don't rely on one and only for all these things. Your love life will be better, more reliable, more spread out, and it will help your intimate relationships as you are coming from a more secure place.

A RELATIONSHIP MAY NOT BE THE ANSWER

A relationship may not be the answer. While a good loving relationship can make both parties happier, a poor relationship can make both parties miserable. If you aren't happy by yourself, you aren't likely to be happy together. If you aren't healthy by yourself, you aren't likely to be healthy together. If you're poor by yourself, you'll stay poor together. If you have personal problems, they require personal solutions, not other people. If the time is not right, it's okay, you can come back to it later.

If you aren't happy with how things are going, don't think love is the cure. It's an easy mistake to make, but it can be a costly mistake. A bad relationship will suck the life out of you. It will take over your time and your mind. It will multiply negative thoughts. It can make you unhealthier, poorer, and unhappier. If you aren't happy, you must go back and follow the steps. Read on but come back and act on this later when you have cared for yourself.

BE YOUR OWN MAN

Be your own man. Do your own thing. Make your own schedule. Keep your own friendships. Do your own hobbies. Work on your own projects. Share some of your time, but not all of it. Less time can be more when it comes to relationships. You are there to support and enrich each other, not to merge into one person doing the same thing all the time. She wants a strong man who does his own thing. That's who she is initially attracted to and it's important you keep doing it. Give her time, attention, affection, and love, but also keep space to give those things to yourself too.

A common problem in love relationships is too much. Too much time together. Too much overlap. Too much shared. It usually doesn't start this way but can creep up on you slowly. Your time together is so good that you just keep spending more and more of it together. Careful! You need space apart to grow individually so you can come together and share. It's a dance. It's a balance. Just make sure that you're keeping time for yourself every day. You're not planning all around her. You're making plans for yourself around the things you have to do, enjoy doing, and make you feel good about yourself.

You can be her man while also being your own man. You can give her love without smothering her. You can spend time together and spend time apart. You can be dependable and reliable to her while still making time to do your own thing. It will keep things healthy for longer and make your time together that much more precious.

RIGHT PERSON, RIGHT PLACE, RIGHT TIME

Right person, right place, right time. The odds of this all coming together at once isn't all that likely, so if it does happen be very grateful, and if not you may need to compromise. Maybe you meet the right person, but it's in the wrong place. If you haven't yet found the best place for you and are traveling soon, the relationship can't go too far. Maybe she's leaving. Maybe you pass her in the airport terminal and it's just not meant to be. Even if you meet in the right place, the timing might be wrong. You might be at different life stages. Maybe she's in a relationship or you're coming out of one. And even if you find yourself in the right place at the right time, the person you meet isn't right. The match isn't quite good enough or there's too much value mismatch. If everything aligns, you've hit the jackpot but that's not normally how it happens so you may have to compromise on person, place, or time.

Depending on where you are in your life it may be better to sit this one out, work on your life, and wait to get to the right place and time. Love doesn't need to wait for perfect conditions though. It's okay to get started now, knowing that it's all temporary anyways. Starting in the wrong place is not ideal, but it's okay. Starting at the wrong time is not ideal, but it's okay. Even starting with the wrong person can be okay. It doesn't have to be perfect to have value. It doesn't have to last forever to be worth experiencing. The important thing is to not force it. If it's the wrong person, at the wrong place, at the wrong time, it's much better to wait and build. But if you have enough favorable conditions, give it a try. It doesn't have to be perfect and it's hard to make it all work. Keep trying though, because if you get the trinity of right person, right place, right time, you're in a great position to have a long lasting and fulfilling love relationship.

BE DEPENDABLE

Be dependable. Be reliable. Be someone people can count on. Be someone she can count on. This doesn't mean you have to be around all the time. It doesn't mean you're at her beck and call. It means you're someone who follows through on your own plans. You are a man of your word. You get up every day and go to work. It makes you someone she can plan around. She can gauge your trajectory. She knows you'll follow through. She'll be able to depend on you and any future kids will be able to depend on you. It first and foremost means you can depend on yourself. You'll come through for yourself. A lot of people can't do this and they will fall by the wayside. But you'll still be here because of your dependability and people will seek your side.

The average person is not dependable. They aren't reliable. They can't count on themselves so other people can't count on them. They don't do as they say. Their plans fall through. They get distracted and give up easily. They call in sick to work. The problem is with themselves but affects everyone around them. People can't make solid plans with them, because they may flake. It's hard to make life plans with them because who knows what they will do. It's not conducive to loving relationships and people seek to avoid.

Try to be dependable, especially to yourself. Follow through on your daily habits. They matter a lot. Do your workouts. Eat your good food. Breathe. Review your goals. Commit acts of love. Be someone you can count on for yourself. So when you make plans with others you and everyone knows you'll be there. Be someone others can depend on and they will want to plan around you.

FIGURE OUT WHAT YOU WANT

Figure out what you want. Do you want a strong love relationship? Do you just want sex? Do you want experience? Do you want someone to talk to who will understand you? Do you want a warm body to cuddle with? Do you want a cheerleader? Do you want a life partner? Do you want an adventure partner? Do you want a work partner? Do you want someone to start a family with? Do you want someone to share affection with? If you want some of these things but not the others, that's fine. The important thing is that you know what you want. If you don't know what you want there will be a lot of confusion and hurt. You aren't too likely to get what you want. But if you take the time to figure out what you want there's a good chance you can get it.

To figure out what you want you have to be honest with yourself. Listen to your gut. Listen to your heart. Study your desires. Pay attention to your cravings. Get specific. If it changes over time, that's normal, but watch the changes. If it feels selfish or limited, it's okay for now. Don't judge yourself for what you want. It's okay. You need to know so you can try to go out and get it.

Knowing what you want will save you from a lot of trauma and drama. If you want love from someone who isn't going to give it to you, you should know that early on so you can do something else. If you want sex from someone who isn't going to give it to you, save yourself the time. To do this you'll have to also figure out what she wants which is a bit more difficult. But the important thing for now is figuring out what you want so you can try for it.

GO TALK TO HER

Go talk to her. Make a move. Introduce yourself. Express your interest. She may ignore you or move away from you, but at least you know you tried. If you never tried you never had a chance. If you never introduced yourself you'll be mad you didn't try. When you try, there's a chance she's into you and maybe something can happen. Relationships always start with two strangers. Maybe there is a mutual or online introduction, but there's a point where neither of you know each other and it's up to you to change that. You may be a perfect match or you might not. But you will only find out if you go talk to her.

You have to have some courage and perspective. Many people are too scared to approach and it's usually because they have the wrong perspective. They don't understand the risks and rewards. They think the risk of getting blown out is bad. Never trying is a guaranteed failure! Try spending a lifetime alone and dying without family. The reward is high. Finding love and building a family has to happen somehow. It's up to you.

You must go talk to her. It's simple. Nothing too bad can happen and a lot good can happen. It takes some men way too long to learn this lesson. Some never learn it. They think maybe there's a way around it. Not really. There's way more than enough men. Men are born in higher supply. You can check the census. No one is going to look for you in your room if you stay in there. It's up to you to beat the odds. You have to go out there and be social even if it's scary. It's scarier to never do anything. It's got to start somewhere. So when you see her, go talk to her!

FIGURE OUT WHAT SHE WANTS

Figure out what she wants. She might want you, she might not. She might want your things. She might want to be loved. She might just want sex. She might want to be seen. She might want someone who understands her. She might want a warm body. There's a lot of things she could want and she might not want the rest of the bunch. Figuring out what she wants is pivotal before proceeding in the relationship. Knowing what she wants will tell you if it makes sense to go deeper. It tells you if it will be casual or serious, short term or long term, open or closed. Figuring out what you want is easy, but a lot of it will be up to her, so figure out what she wants.

You can start by asking her what she wants. You can continue by asking her what she wants. Ask her what she wants out of a relationship with you. Ask her what she wants right now. She will probably tell you, although she might not actually know. In any case, you can't read her mind, although you will be able to glean from her actions. Pay attention to her. See what she responds to. Look for her face to light up. Let her get her way and see what that is. She will let you know what she wants, whether she knows it or not.

If you read this wrong it can cause a lot of friction in the relationship. If one person wants love and the other person just wants sex it will cause pain and confusion if both parties aren't aware. That's just one example of many possibilities. Try to get on the same page. You don't have to have the exact same goals- a relationship is a trade. But if you don't know what she wants you can't make a proper trade. Figure out what she wants, and if you want to give it to her, give it to her. She'll be satisfied.

LEARN HER LOVE LANGUAGE

Learn her love language. There are many ways to express love. She may respond best to a certain kind of love. She may be uncomfortable with other kinds of love. The basic love languages are gifts, quality time, words of affirmation, acts of service, and physical touch. You don't have to speak the exact same love language, but it's good to know what she responds to best. Give her more of that and less of the rest. She will feel loved in a way that is comfortable to her.

Some people like to hear words of affirmation like "I love you". Some people are uncomfortable hearing and responding to that. It may have to do with not feeling it, or it may have to do with childhood experiences. Some people like to receive gifts, others are uncomfortable receiving. Some like to spend quality time doing fun activities together, some people are homebodies that like to read. Some people like to exchange physical touch more than others. Some people are less comfortable with it. Some express their love through acts of devotion, some don't do many favors but it doesn't mean they don't feel it. It's good to know your own love language, but also important to know hers. You don't want to give her love that she isn't equipped to receive. You want to give her love that works for her.

You can ask for her love language or you can observe her. Maybe she is very encouraging and that would suggest she speaks affirmations. Maybe she is very touchy and that suggests she speaks touch. These are a few of many signs you can observe. You can also learn through experimentation. Speak to her in all the love languages and see what she responds to best. See what she reciprocates, see what she stays away from. If she doesn't reciprocate, it may just mean that's not her language. If she does, you're speaking her language. Try them all out and see what works best. Mix it up but stick with the winners. She will be more comfortable with love this way. It won't feel forced to her. She'll be able to speak her natural love language with you.

GET ON THE SAME PAGE

Get on the same page. Figure out what you want, figure out what she wants, and communicate. You don't have to have the exact same wants and needs, if there's some overlap. Focus on the overlap and build around that. If you want to have kids together, awesome. If you want to have casual sex, that's fine too. If you both want an adventure partner, now you can make plans. If you aren't on the same page people will get hurt. Get clear about what each of you wants and go for it.

If you both want all the same things, that's awesome, but it's not necessary. Most relationships don't work that way. Some of them have limited depth, but that doesn't mean they aren't pursuing. And if they do have limited depth, at least you know now before you invest too much emotion and energy into it. And you can let her know how you feel to save her from the same. It's important.

You might find yourselves on the same page in the same book. Or you might be on the same page in different books. That's okay, so long as you know as early as you can. Love hurts so take precaution. Love that is limited in depth is okay too. Just be clear with each other by getting on the same page.

FACE THE SAME DIRECTION

Face the same direction. It's more important that you face the same direction than you face each other. You don't need to mirror each other. You should have an overlapping vision for the future that includes each other, or it's probably not going to even work in the short term. You don't have to see the exact same thing, but you should be at least facing in the same direction.

Talk about future plans. Talk about future possibilities. Talk about future predictions. You want to enjoy your time in the moment but it's good to get on the same page about the future. Do you see yourself in the same location? Do you see yourself together? What do you see each other working on? If you are facing in different directions, towards different locations, towards different lifestyles, you are probably also facing towards different people and it won't last.

Talk about it early on. You don't have to have the exact same vision to make it work. But it's important that you see even the possibility of being together to make it work in the short term, otherwise it won't be compelling to either of you. Talk to her and see if you can hold hands and walk in the same direction together.

KNOW PORN AND MASTURBATION

Know porn and masturbation. These are tools that can be abused to degrade your relationships. Or they can be tools to help you stay non-needy and faithful. It's all in the understanding and how you use it. Strategic moderation beats both excess and abstinence. If you use these tools wrong they will cause you problems but used right they can enrich your relationships.

First, masturbation. In the short span of a couple days, sexual relief is a want, not a need. Excessive masturbation is unnecessary and will sap your energy. Over weeks and months, sexual relief is more of a need. For short term reward, masturbation is not the best tool. You can build it up for a week or more and it will boost your testosterone and energy. But as a long term personally independent solution for sexual desire, masturbation is a great tool. You don't want to be totally reliant on anyone else to fulfill your sexual needs. If you try to go no fap you will become needy and desperate for others. You will pressure her too much. If you can take care of yourself, you can make yourself available but leave it up to her. Even in a long term committed relationship she won't always be available to you. She may not be in the right mood or frame of mind. It may have nothing to do with you. If you can take care of yourself it will let her do her own thing and you won't have to go out seeking anyone else. In this case masturbation will help you stay faithful and non-distracted.

Porn is more complicated. You can think of it as a visual / audio aid to masturbation. Be careful with this. It's shown to change the brain and can have negative effects with your relationships with women. You don't want to get used to seeing them as sexual objects. If porn makes it easier for you to get necessary relief then sure. If it helps you stay faithful then okay. If it's part of a daily routine, then it's bad for you. You don't need porn if you're aren't masturbating. And you don't even need porn to masturbate. It's an extra tool to be used strategically and sparingly.

Masturbation and porn are important issues for men especially. Too many damage their energy, minds, social lives, and intimate relationships by failing to understand and use these tools. Many men overuse and abuse for short term entertainment. It's okay for necessary relief, independence, non-distraction and faithfulness. Understand and make the most of it. It can hurt you or it can help you.

COMMITMENT BEATS FREEDOM

Commitment beats freedom. The idea of freedom is great. You can do anything you want! Except having a strong committed relationship. This requires commitment. Commitment may close some doors, but it will open one important door to love. Free love works much better in theory than in practice. Love requires trust and trust requires commitment. If you can't commit, you may have some fun, but you will limit yourself in the most important way.

At some point you will have to make a commitment. It depends on what you want. You may want variety and experience starting off. But eventually you will want stability and the ability to start a family. This requires commitment. And you will have to commit to someone who has annoying flaws. It's hard to make this sacrifice, but eventually it's necessary. It does matter who you make commitments with, but in the end it's important that it was someone. Your true soulmate may be out there, but you could spend a lifetime and never find her. It's better to go with the person who feels right and makes sense. She doesn't have to have everything and you don't have to have everything together. There can be problems and that's okay. The important thing is that you can make the same commitment and work forward on your goals together.

COMPROMISE BEATS ULTIMATUMS

Compromise beats ultimatums. Don't say "it's my way or the highway". Don't try to change her behavior forever. Don't say how things absolutely have to be. This is a good way to lose love. It's a good way to continuously break up or establish uncomfortable power dynamics. It's much better to compromise. She isn't going to be perfect. Your relationship isn't going to be perfect. She will have some bad habits. The relationship will have some flaws. It's okay because perfect isn't out there. Learn to live with each other's problems. Everyone has a package of good and bad and you're signing up for that together. Don't put that massive fork in the road unless you want to go walk it alone. Instead, learn to compromise.

Compromise comes handy in arguments. You can stand up for yourself while being agreeable too. You don't have to be right. You just need these issues resolved. Part of compromise means sacrificing your position and saying it's okay. Learn to be okay with imperfection. You can't fix your relationship and you can't fix her. You can make things better by playing your part. You should communicate what you want but differentiate it from what you need. You don't need much and you will want a lot of things you can't have. Forget it. Don't make ultimatums or permanent demands.

Compromise. Make the most of what you have. It won't work perfect but it will work better.

STUDY HER

Study her. Study what she's about. Study what she wants. Study her behavior. Study her history. This doesn't mean you have to stalk her. But do your due diligence. If you're going to go far with someone you must have the information to make a good decision. If you don't study her you may not discover a massive problem until it's too late. If you do, you can avoid these problems. If you study her you can also make sure you are on the same page, learn her love language, learn what she likes, and give these things to her. If you don't study her you will be oblivious. You aren't likely to ace a test you don't study for so if you want to ace relationships you ought to study them.

Study people in general. Study women. Study evolutionary psychology. Study some human biology. Read the sorts of books and watch the sorts of things women are into. To master a subject you must come at it from all angles. You must take it seriously and be studious. Like most things you will learn a lot from experience. So study your interactions with her and give it some time to digest later. You would spend the time to analyze your business and health, so you should spend the same time to analyze your relationships too. Put in the time and study hard. You will score much better with women and have better relationships.

BREATHE WITH HER

Breathe with her. Slow down. Pay attention to her. Get on the same page as her body. Take deep breaths together. It will bring you close and help you understand each other. It will reduce anxiety and arguments. Deep breathing will have a strong calming and comforting effect. It's easy to run on and on with nervous energy. Or forget about her and talk about you. Or forget about her and think about what you want to do with her. To breathe with her you have to pay attention to her. Not many people will do this. She might not have learned it. She will appreciate it.

Communication is more nonverbal than verbal. The words are important, but the body speaks its own language. The body communicates through posture, heartbeat, skin, and breath. Breatheis something that is easy to sense and take control of. You can talk and talk and struggle to get on the same page if you aren't paying attention to what the body is saying. Or you can say nothing at all and totally understand each other if you have a good sense for each other's bodies.

When you see her it's a good idea to take a moment to breathe, especially if you're keyed up about something. Invite her to breathe with you. Take awareness of each other. Sense the energy being exchanged. Relax into it. Verbal communication after this point will go smoother, if it's needed at all. Or you can go deeper with each other's bodies, connecting movement with the breath, and even pleasure with the breath. You will better be able to understand each other. Give it a try- breathe with her. It will be awesome.

GIVE HER SOME POWER

Give her some power. Let her reject you. Put yourself out there and give her the option. Put a shot up in her area and see if she rejects it or hits it back to you. You can try to read the signs but you can't read her mind. Take things 75% of the way and let her finish the job. If she goes for it, she goes for it, if she doesn't, she doesn't, and now you know. If she chooses to reject you, it's okay. It may be temporary, it may be mood dependent. If she rejects you over and over, that's okay, it's time to move on and there are more options for you out there. If you don't give her any power, you are taking her power from her. Let her be a woman. Let her have some power over you.

You can be a strong man and give her power at the same time. A strong man and a strong woman go together. You can try to take from her with brute force but it will end badly for everyone. Either ask her if you can proceed or lie on your back and let her finish the job, metaphorically or for real. Maybe she does, maybe she doesn't, but now you know.

Give her some power, but not all the power. There needs to be a balance. Don't wait for her to initiate. That's your job as the man. Don't wait by her side at her beck and call. That's the job of a servant. Do your own thing. Be your own man. Sometimes you need to leave her side. Sometimes you need to pull away. Sometimes you need to tell her "no" or "not right now". But some of the times you need to put yourself out there and see what she does with her power.

MAKE YOURSELF VULNERABLE

Make yourself vulnerable to her. Open up to her. Let her see who you really are. Tell her your full story. Expose your belly. She may stab you or decide to stay away from you. That's a risk. But she's going to find out sooner or later and it's better to make yourself vulnerable sooner so she can decide. She'll have a chance to relate to the real you. To see you for who you are. If she sees your vulnerability and is okay with it, you're in a good position for things to last.

You don't need to open up early or all at once. But it's gotta happen sooner or later. Without vulnerability, there can't be close connection. If she doesn't stab your exposed belly, it builds trust. Trust is crucial to relationships. If you can see each other's worst and be okay with that you can be real with each other. So let your guard down. Break down some walls. Tell her what's hard to tell anyone. See how she responds. She may love you more for it.

KEEP IT TO YOURSELF

Keep it to yourself. Having good communication doesn't mean you have to share everything with her. You don't have to share all your doubts and fears. You don't have to share your negative emotions towards her. You don't have to share what you perceive to be her shortcomings. These things don't make her life better. It's good to have transparent communication but not at the cost of being a dick and stirring up unnecessary drama. Keep it to yourself. These are your own issues. Resolve them yourself. You can talk about them afterwards but you don't have to because it's still not helpful and you'll have it handled yourself.

It's tempting to share everything you're feeling as you grow closer. It's true that open communication is good as a generality, but not in every case. Don't forget that your job is to make her life better. You are supposed to be her rock. You are supposed to lift her up and inspire her. You might not be able to do this every time but you can take some space instead to do your own thing and resolve your own issues. You don't have to work through everything with her. Your own negative issues should be worked through by yourself. You're not each other's therapists. Open communication is not an excuse to let her know what you think is wrong with her. Keep these things to yourself.

Share the good stuff instead. You want a high ratio of good interactions to bad interactions. The pleasant times should far outweigh the unpleasant times. Don't manufacture extra unpleasant situations when you don't have to. For some reason it can be natural to stir up drama, but that doesn't mean that it's right. Take a step back, take a deep breathe, and keep it to yourself. You have your own problems and they don't need to be shared with others. She will be glad that you're not coming at her with so many problems. If you do, you will make her life worse off and she will be gone for it. Focus on helping her and keep your doubts to yourself.

PLAY THE MOUSE TO HER CAT

Play the mouse to her cat. Let her queen capture your king. Just because she's elusive doesn't mean she's not a predator. She wants to pursue too. Cats are skittish but they still like to kill their meat. Let her play the game. Express your feelings and intentions but give her the space to come after you. The choice is hers. The cat didn't go too far looking for the mouse. The mouse came near her place and made its presence known. Give her a ball she can hit but make her take a swing too because that's what she wants.

It's good to be bold and somewhat aggressive. The timid never make their feelings or presence known and are overlooked. The bold don't always win, but they maximize their shots and their odds. You don't want to be reckless though. You want to be persistent and you will have to convince her. But she wants to work a little bit too. Make it easy, but not that easy. Let her know she can score but make her run the ball.

Playing the mouse to her cat is a roleplay that respects her animal. It will keep you in the right frame of mind. You can play it wrong- do too little and never get noticed; do too much and drive her away. Do as the mouse who is captured by the cat. He finds her and makes his presence known. The mouse does much of the work but in the end, the cat chooses. Let her pounce on you.

RESPECT HER INNER ANIMAL

Respect her inner animal. She's an animal. She's wild. She's going to be impulsive. She's going to be moody sometimes. What she wants will change depending on the time of the day or the time of the month. Animals will be animals. Don't be mad about it. Respect it.

Animals aren't always logical. Animals aren't robots either. Animals do what they want. They think about it, but they rationalize afterwards. Animals will take advantage of other animals. Animals will hurt other animals. Animals will hunt other animals. She will do all these things. Remind yourself that it's not about you. She's doing her own thing. She's being an animal.

Animals have needs. They need shelter, food, and warmth. They need sex from time to time. Animals want companionship but they don't necessarily need love. Give her these things when she needs them. Be ready to serve her inner animal. Her animal needs will change at different times. She won't need you all the time. She might not need you at all. But when she does need you, be ready to satisfy her inner animal.

RESPECT HER CYCLE

Respect her cycle. She's changing. The wave is coming in our out. The moon's face is coming and going. Winter follows spring. There is expansion and contraction. She's going to feel differently at different times. She's going to feel differently about you. She may not like you every day. She might not be nice to you today. It may be something you could have done better, or it might just be the season. Try to understand her. Don't take it too personally. It won't last forever. It's okay for now. The tide will flow out and summer will come again.

It's too easy to get caught up in arguments and criticisms about minor details. Those small things do matter, but they're part of a bigger picture. It's colored by mood and emotion. Sometimes it's stormy, sometimes it's sunny. You can take the feedback and grow from it. Don't let yourself get too hot, make hasty decisions or ultimatums. Give it some time. While you can make it easier by taking the right actions, it will also heal with time.

Appreciate the good weather. It won't last forever. This may be the last for a while, or forever. It certainly won't be forever. Don't take her for granted during this time. Too many people don't bring an umbrella because they think it will always be sunny. Amplify your love. Be boldly generous. Now is the time to make the most of it.

Pay attention to her month. You'll be much better able to understand her. If you can estimate the dates and see what's coming next it will take much of the surprise out of it. It will take some time to learn her. You will learn when to give her space and when to seek her out. Things will get better and easier over more months. Unpredictability consumes a lot of mental energy so as this becomes more routine it will become smoother and easier. Study her.

The man's hormonal cycle is very flat. There will be some changes, but relatively minor. You are more of a rock. Lower variance. Not as high, not as low. More even loving. It's hard not to catch her emotions when you are very close to her, but you have to try to step back and give her space and time.

Be her rock. Give her some security. Try to grin through the winter. The spring will come back around.

MAKE HER LIFE BETTER

Make her life better. Don't make her life worse. Make her life better in as many areas as you can. Make your intention to make her life better. Take actions to make her life better. If you do this, her life will improve with your help and she will be happy about it. Satisfying relationships improve the lives of both parties. Enduring relationships are mutually beneficial. Aim to improve her life and you will make for a good relationship.

Don't forget that you're supposed to be making her life better. You may get too caught up in what you're getting out of it. Or you get irritable over small things. You might try to change her behavior to suit you better. These things tend to make her life worse, not better. If you make her life worse she will resent you and create space between you. If you make her life worse she should leave you, and eventually she will. Don't forget that it's your job in the relationship to help her.

Making her life better can mean a variety of things. It might mean being someone who gives her love and affection. It might mean lending her an ear and understanding. It might mean helping her improve her diet. It could mean helping her with her work. It might mean giving her sexual satisfaction. Maybe you add some adventure and excitement to her life. Maybe you are a stable emotional force for her. It could be giving her pleasure. Making her life better can mean a lot of things and it's all about her. If it's about you, it's about what you can do for her. Focus on helping her.

Obviously you should get something out of it as well. You will get plenty just by giving. It's fulfilling and enriching to give. She will return the favor to a degree. But don't expect proportional reciprocation. Don't keep score. Focus on giving, helping, and making her life better and she will find a way to do the same for you.

OPEN JARS FOR HER

Open jars for her. Reach to the top shelf. Carry her heavy bags. Shelter her from the rain with an umbrella. Keep her warm with your body. This is basic man shit. You are big and strong and are there to help her. She is good at being a woman, you are good at being a man. You can help in intellectual and emotional ways as well. But you are a big strong man and that is a service. It may sound funny, but she will appreciate it if you open her jars.

No woman wants a weakling for a man. She may tolerate it if everything else is good enough. But she wants a physically strong man. That doesn't mean you need to be a musclebound gym rat. It means you should be in relatively good shape because you take care of your body. If she opens your jars you may have a problem. She can be healthy and athletic too. That's great. It's not a competition. But the way of the man and the woman is different. The man has the potential for greater strength and length, especially of the upper body. This is a gift for you to help her and you should take advantage of it. It sets something off in her animal brain. It feels good to be around a strong man she can trust. That's you!

GIVE HER GOOD FOOD

Give her food. Feed her good food. Bring good food around her. Pay for her food if she'll let you. She's an animal and animals like to eat. Men have been doing this for all time. Go out and hunt, bring back your spoils, and share it with her. It's not rocket science. By doing this you're also investing in her. If you are going to together for a while you want her to be as healthy as she can be. This doesn't mean trying to change her or force her, it just means helping her. If you're able to do this you'll demonstrate that you'll be a good father as well for providing good food for her children. Whether you want love, sex, or family, it's all the same. Feed her good food.

Take her out to healthy restaurants. Take her out shopping at health food stores. Take her to the farmers market. Stock your house with good food for yourself. Then share with her. You come first. If you aren't healthy, you can't even do this. You have to do the best you can for yourself first. And if you're broke, forget about it. You have to cover your own bases. But once you've got yourself covered this is something important you can bring to the table- good food!

There's something in the animal brain that just loves to be fed. You can do this for her. She'll be happy in the short term, and healthier in the long term. It will set you up for a family and community based on what's most important- good food! So go ahead and feed her.

GIVE HER WARMTH

Give her warmth. Keep her warm emotionally and keep her warm physically. A traditional role of ancient men has been to keep his woman and children warm. He may help with collecting wood and kindling the fire, building a shelter, bedding, and his physical body presence. It can take a lot of energy to stay warm, and this is something you can provide her. Physical heat is a sign of health and abundance. Sick and weak people stay cold and don't have much warmth to share. Offer her your warmth and she will appreciate it.

First you must make yourself warm. You have to prioritize warmth. You must have a good diet to provide you with fuel to burn hot. You need to have proper clothing that keeps you warm. You should be physically active to keep your heat up. You should have a warm bed. Once you are cared for, you can offer her your warmth. Offer to warm her back with your hot hands. Offer to warm her bed with your sleeping body. It's simple, but it goes a long way. She doesn't want to be cold at night. If you can help her with this she will want you around more and cherish your presence in her life.

Physical warmth should come with emotional warmth. Put affection into your hands when you touch her. Put love into her bed when you sleep with her. She could use a space heating robot and get the same thing if you don't give her emotional warmth. Kiss her and give her words of kindness, encouragement, admiration, and love. Compared to the prospect of being cold and alone, a consistent warm loving man will really improve her life.

Not every man can fulfill this role. Some don't have the health to burn hot. Others don't have the wealth for warm clothing. Many don't have the happiness to be consistently emotionally warm. It's not easy. It requires taking charge of your own life. But if you can do this for yourself, you can do this for her. Warm yourself up and use your excess to keep her warm too.

GIVE HER ORGASMS

Give her orgasms. Make her cum. Give her the ultimate physical pleasure. You do this and she will be very happy. She will keep seeking you out for it. This should be obvious but unfortunately is not. Many men are too narcissistic. They model their lovemaking off pornography and focus on their own fantasies and gratification. Forget that. It's way too easy to pleasure yourself. You can make yourself orgasm very easily. It's fun with her help but should not be the focus. Sex is a partner game. Focus on her. Give her pleasure. You make her cum and she will be happy to do the same for you. This one simple intention for lovemaking makes all the difference.

The female orgasm is way beyond the male orgasm. She can cum multiple times, over and over again. She has way more nerve endings in her pleasure centers. Men can't feel too much compared to women. You can see it in her body when she climaxes. It must be an incredible sensation. Which is why it is such a great gift. You can give her so much pleasure.

Female sexuality is different in other ways too. She likes to be teased much more. She likes a longer build up. Why not, when she can feel so much? So tease her. Take your time. Slowly circle into her hot spots. When she thinks you're going to give it to her, make her wait a little more. She'll be that much more ready when you do touch her. Start slow and explore. Listen to how her body responds. If she likes something, do more of it. Build it up. Keep going.

Forget your own parts for a bit. They're not always the best for giving pleasure. Use your hands and your mouth. The cool thing about your hands is that it allows you to use your body for other things. You can create a lot of body contact. You can wrap your legs or arm around her. You can use your mouth on other areas. When you dive down with your mouth it will feel good for her, but you're also far away from her, so it has its advantages and drawbacks. Just keep going until she pushes you away, hopefully after she cums. When she cums, now it's your turn, but not before. You can let her hold you if she wants, but don't let her focus on you until she gets hers.

This stuff should be obvious, but obviously it's not. Which is why if you do it you have such an advantage. She will get a lot from you and it will be hard to replace you. It may lead to love or it may just feel good. Either way it will help make your relationship with her great.

WRITE HER LETTERS

Write her letters. No one writes letters anymore. She probably doesn't get any letters. But she probably wants them. Writing her a letter is a simple but sweet act that is very appreciated. You can make it cute, you can make it affectionate, you can make it sentimental. It's something private for her to read. It's a memento for her to keep. It's a reminder of you. It's something real that she can touch and feel. You can mail it to her or you can sneak it somewhere she'll find it. She will love it.

Make your letter fun. It shouldn't be too serious. It definitely shouldn't be something that needs to be communicated in person. It should be something extra. Express your emotion, your thanks, your gratitude. Share a funny story. Try to make her laugh. Throw in a little drawing or a small memento to go with it. It's a very small act that will go a long way. So write her a letter!

IT'S BETTER TO GIVE THAN TO RECEIVE

It's better to give than to receive. It feels great to give, and it's under your control. It feels good to receive too, but it's not totally under your control. Giving is up to you, receiving is not. Giving is something you can do and feel good about on the daily. If you receive, that's cool too, but it shouldn't be the goal- it's a byproduct of giving. Focus on how you can give more and much of the rest will take care of itself.

Give selectively. You can't give everything to everyone. You must be picky with your resources-your time, energy, attention, affection, love, and money. Be careful about what you give and who you give it to. Don't give indiscriminately and infinitely.

Be generous to a point. Not everyone deserves your energy. You may have an abundance but you don't have an infinite supply. Give to the people you care about. These people are likely to return the favor as well. It's not the goal, but it's nice when it comes back your way.

Not everyone has much to give. People are too stressed out about their physical health, their work, and short on their own happiness. When coming from a place of scarcity you will be more interested in what you can receive. But when you have provided for yourself you'll be able to turn outward with your giving. When you are rich yourself you don't need to receive. Take care of yourself and you'll be ready to turn outward to give.

DON'T KEEP SCORE

Don't keep score. It's not a competition. It's not a balance sheet. Every good deed must not be repaid in kind. Every bad deed need not be remembered. It's easy to stop giving because you aren't receiving as much as you like. It's also easy to try to get even on things. Neither is a good approach. Forgive the bad stuff. Resolve it on your own time. Keep on giving. You don't need to receive back 1 to 1. If you want to give, just give.

The great thing about giving is that it's under your control. While it feels great to receive, it's not up to you. Giving feels good too. Don't let imbalance stop you from giving. Things will swing back your way eventually. And if not, at least you can say you gave it your all. If you hold back and wait because of imbalance, the flow will stop and that's it. It may never start flowing again. So just keep on giving whatever the score is. It will keep the love flowing.

SHOW HER YOU LOVE HER

Show her you love her. Perform acts of love for her. You don't have to tell her you love her. She may want this, she may not. She might not be ready. That might not be her love language. But you can show her that you love her. She may not be ready or even want that, but it gives both of you the opportunity to find out. Give her affection. Give her love. Spend quality time with her. Give her back rubs. Give her gifts. Give her words of affirmation. Think about what you can do to help her and do that.

Everyone wants to feel loved. Not everyone wants to be told they are loved all the time. She might or she might not. It's a lot of pressure. Small words of affirmation and small favors are way less pressure and they get the job done. She will notice and appreciate. She will get a warm feeling in her gut. It will give her a chance to feel loved and reciprocate if she chooses to. A loving relationship should stay loving. You never lock in love forever, except in perhaps some parent child relationships. You have to keep earning love and you do this by performing acts of love.

PROTECT HER BUT DON'T TRAP HER

Protect her but don't trap her. Keep her safe but not caged. She should feel comfortable around you. But if she feels trapped she will want to run. If she feels caged she will break out. Give her enough freedom so she feels like she's still choosing you. Don't make her feel stuck. Guard her from danger but empower her to be her own person with her own space. She will feel good to pick you.

Watch her back for danger. There are wild threats in the jungles and the streets. You should be strong and prepared to fight these animals. Protect her from threats to her health and her wellbeing. You should be well endowed with strength and finances to help provide a safety net. Being in that position is something to be proud of. You took care of your health, wealth, and happiness and now can help with hers.

Too much vigilance will make her feel trapped. Don't prevent her from going on her own. Do your own things. Don't try to read her private messages. Think your own thoughts. Don't threaten her or make her feel unsafe. If you make her feel loved by someone special she will fly back to nest with you. If you break her wings she will plot an escape. Let her be her own person and you be your own person. Protect her person, give her freedom, and she will love you for it.

GIVE HER SPACE

Give her space. Don't try to spend all the time with her. She's her own person. She needs room to grow on her own. You need room to grow on your own. You separate, you come together. That's the dance of a relationship. Don't worry what she's up to. Let her do her own thing. If you crowd her space too much she'll be gone. Give her some space and she'll be back.

It's normal to worry over her, but that doesn't mean it's productive. Negative emotions and need to control are destructive to any relationship. You can't watch her all the time, and you shouldn't have to if you have something good. You can't spend all the time with her and why would you want to? The more time apart the more you learn different things, the more you can come together to share and support each other. It's a delicate balance. Too much time together and the relationship stagnates. Too much time apart and there's no relationship. The key is in coming back together.

You need space to do your own thing too. You need your time to train, to learn, and to grow. You get diminishing returns on time spent together. It may be fun, comfortable, and feel good, but that doesn't mean it's good for you. You have to be your own man and work on your own projects. So give her some space because you need some too.

DON'T TRY TO CHANGE HER, BUT BE WILLING TO CHANGE FOR HER

Don't try to change her but be willing to change for her. Take her as she is. Hopefully she grows, maybe she doesn't. No one likes it when you try to change them. She is how she is. On the other hand, it's good to be willing to change for her. Making sacrifice and adjustment is a strong act of commitment. There's no shame in growth. The best people change throughout their lives. One of the benefits of having a partner is the intimate feedback you will receive. Some of it will be nice cheerleading, some of it may come across as annoying nagging. Either way, there's value there. Don't pressure her. But listen to what she says and you will grow faster over time.

There's a myth that a perfect loving relationship accepts each other exactly as they are. Perfect isn't real and it usually doesn't work out this way. We do need to make some compromise on what we're willing to accept. But you shouldn't be enabling mediocrity. Everyone has room to grow. No one should stay the same. If there are problem behaviors they need to be pointed out and adjustments should be made over time. Good behavior should be complimented to be reinforced over time. The feedback may hurt at times, but it leads to faster growth.

You should be willing to change, but you shouldn't expect her to either. Take her as she is. She won't be happy being pressured to be someone she isn't. Help her grow by focusing on the things she's doing well. Make your feedback gentle. She may change over time, she may not. If you were down with her from the start it won't matter too much. Expecting her to change is hard on her but it will be hard on you as well. You may be disappointed as nothing happens and the friction increases. She's not your Pokémon to level up. Let her be her and love her for it.

STAND FOR YOUR VALUES

Stand for your values. Don't back down on the important stuff, even if it's coming from her. She wants a strong man, not a butler. You should be generous with her, agreeable, and willing to change for her. But growth doesn't mean fundamental change. There are certain core values deep inside you that are fundamental to you. They are your unique view of the world. Over time these may adjust with new information, but you can't force it. Changing a belief is not like changing a habit. Sheer willpower of repression can't be permanent. Don't try to change these. Believe in them. Stand behind them. Show her that you are solid.

You don't have to have the same view as her on everything. You don't have to agree on everything. Differences don't have to cause arguments. The goal isn't to be the same. You can celebrate difference, or at the least compromise for it. She would rather you be your own person with your own rock steady beliefs. This shows her you won't back down under other people's pressure. You should demonstrate your ability to be flexible with people, and part of that is agreeing to disagree. You may not stand the same on everything. Be ok with that.

DON'T TAKE HER FOR GRANTED

Don't take her for granted. She could be gone tomorrow. You could be gone tomorrow. Emotions can change quick. Just because things are great right now doesn't mean they will be forever. Don't get too comfortable and assume you're locked in forever. It could be gone soon, especially if you forget to put in the love and effort to keep it going. Appreciate what you have right now and keep loving like you just started.

We can forget how precarious the balance of love can be. Our focus drifts towards other things, which is fine. Or we try to shape things in a certain way forgetting how good it already is. Things don't need to be changed if it's already good. If it's not broke, don't fix it. Don't come in with your negative emotions because it's not perfect. It was never perfect and can never be perfect. Appreciate what you do have. It's magic and it may just be a short time. Make the most of it.

Thank her. Tell her you appreciate her in your life. Tell her you're not taking her for granted. Show her by coming back to shower her with love. Keep trying to make her life better. Do your best. One way or another, you will eventually lose each other. Maybe sooner or later. But if you don't take it for granted at least you won't have to regret not appreciating what you had. Enjoy it while you have it.

IT'S TEMPORARY

It's temporary. It won't last forever. It can't last forever. Death is guaranteed to end things, but time may split it up much sooner. It could be over before you know it. This may have been the last. If it keeps on going, the quality will change. Some things will improve, some things will get worse. You may grow together, you may grow apart. Don't expect eternal love. Be happy for the good moments. Don't take them for granted. Appreciate them. There aren't too many and you never know when it's over.

Security and comfort is nice, but too much leads to taking things for granted. It's nice to have a stable relationship built on shared values and fun experiences. But as solid as things seem, it doesn't mean it will always stay that way. Things change.

New experiences change things. New people enter the picture. It's okay. It's better to have love and lost than to never have loved at all. There will likely be more opportunities to love. Or not, because everything is temporary.

Make the most of it. Keep making the most of it. Keep giving and loving. It's on you to keep winning it. If you think you have it then it will faster slip through your grasp. It's never locked in forever. You have to keep putting in work to maintain and grow. In the end, you will lose it, but that's okay. Hopefully you will be able to love again. Appreciate what you have.

MAKE THINGS RIGHT

Make things right. Correct mistakes. You are going to fuck up. It's inevitable. If you look closely you will make mistakes every day. It's impossible to play perfect. You can try your best but the best you can do is try to make things right. Learn your lessons and wait for the next opportunity to do it correctly. You can apologize but you may have to wait for your chance to act. You might not even be able to make things right with the person you wronged. You can fix it by not continuing to wrong the next person. Most of all your mistakes will hurt yourself so it's up to you to make things right to yourself. Make your best effort to do a better job next time and you will.

Most people can't correct mistakes because they can't even identify them. They don't take responsibility for their situation and blame other people for their poor interactions. When things go wrong it's your fault. If you get a bad reaction it's your fault. Take responsibility. Look for things you did wrong and think about how you can do better next time. Let her know you care by saying something or just doing the right thing next time. With this attitude your conduct will get better and better and your results will get better and better. But don't think you will get so good you will play it perfect all the time. Your mistakes will get more nuanced and complicated. Keep looking for them, admitting them, and seeing what you can do better. Make things right. You will be appreciated for this.

FORGIVE HER

Forgive her. Give her more chances. Nobody is perfect. She's allowed to make mistakes without losing everything. It can be way better but there's still no such thing as a perfect relationship. There will at times be friction. Feelings are temporary. Wait on permanent decisions. Find it in your heart to forgive. You will at times lose love but it's likely to come back. Give it time. Healing will happen.

It's much harder to walk around with resentment in your heart. It's much lighter to let it go and just keep on loving. If this requires loving from afar, sometimes loving from afar is appropriate. But it will contribute to loving from near because you're creating more chances for love.

Keep your heart open. Don't close it even if you get pushed away. It's more painful to hate. It feels better to love. It may bring you together or keep you together. Think about how much you'd like to be forgiven. Forgiveness is powerful for love.

GOOD THINGS TAKE TIME

Good things take time. A good relationship takes time. It's a slow process. Don't expect to get everything overnight. If you rush things they tend to break or regress. It will require hours, weeks, months, and even years. Good things don't happen overnight. Enjoy the process. Keep building over time. Things will change. Surprises will happen. Moods and emotions will change. It's all part of the process. More time, better things.

You can't rush closeness. You can't force connection. You can try, and it might even work for a while. But these things take time. Love happens at its own pace. Love grows. A seedling grows into a sapling grows into a tree grows into a forest. This is a long process. There will be predators, pests, fires, and chainsaws. But let it keep going. It will grow over time.

Log the hours. Log the weeks. Log the years. Keep putting in the time. Keep on loving. Keep on serving. Keep on doing the best you can. If you make a mistake today, it's okay. If you lose a battle, that's fine. Play for the long game. Correct your mistakes and try to win the big picture. It will be worth it in the long run, because good things take time.

LOVE HER ANYWAYS

Love her anyways. She's not going to be perfect. No one is perfect. She's going to make mistakes. She's going to do some dumb shit from time to time. She doesn't want to be seen as perfect because that's not real. We all want to have our flaws seen and have them considered forgivable. To hear that although we're not perfect, it's still okay. She's going to have some bad habits. She's going to have some flaws. It's okay, you can love her anyways.

The goal isn't a perfect relationship with a perfect partner. The goal is to have a loving relationship despite these imperfections. It requires acceptance and forgiveness. You have to accept the whole- all the good and the bad. You have to forgive the whole- all the good and the bad.

It's so easy to fixate on all the negatives. On the things we want to change. The things we think should be different. The things we don't like. The annoying behaviors. It's not helpful though. You can see them without being bothered by them. She won't necessarily change, and that's okay. See the whole person. See the bad but focus on the good. You can still love her anyways.

KEEP ON LOVING

Keep on loving. It feels good to love. Let it flow. Keep sending it out into the universe. Even if you get nothing back. Even if you get rejected. Even if you get hurt. Even if what you have falls apart. Keep on loving and love again right away if you stop. It feels good to love and will bring love back your way sooner. It can't hurt so keep on loving.

Many people give up on giving love. They get cynical. They don't want to share it. They become afraid. Others are too busy keeping score. They'll give love when they receive it. They keep on waiting and the love doesn't flow. Others never even get to love because their physiological health isn't in order, they hate their work, and are unhappy. Sure, it would be nice to receive eternal love, but that's just not how it works. Your mom will love you but even that is temporary. You can't depend on the universe to supply you with love. But giving it is your decision. You can keep on giving it as much as you like.

Life is too short to be cold and hurt for long. Whether you are single or in a relationship it will make your life better to give love. It is an energy you can share. It's much easier to give when you have your life for yourself. You will have a full cup of love to pour from, if you love yourself first. It feels good and it won't hurt you. So go ahead and keep on loving.

LOVE

Made in the
USA
Monee, IL